First published January 2016 by Bunny Picnic

ISBN: 978-0-9572754-2-3

To contact the author, email gez@bunnypicnic.co.uk

The author very gratefully acknowledges the help, support and / or inspiration of the following people in the production of this book:

Hannah, Dylan and Louise at Proximity, Bryony and Louise at Group M, John, Angus and Carolyn at Editions, Alex Raybould, Sheillee Kataria, Jake Johnson, Helen Ballard, Lloyd Fletcher, Chris Lightfoot, Joanne Schofield, Daddy Teacha, Dub Judah, Jamie Catto and David Hoyle.

Babylon a fall!

Release Notes

This book is being written using an agile, iterative approach, so like a piece of software, we need some way of tracking which version of it you're currently reading, and any changes in this version compared with the previous version.

As a result, below are the release notes for the version of the book you see before you now.

This book is version number:	1.0.0
Major new features added to this version:	This is the original release of the book. All features are new.
Minor enhancements added to this version:	N/a.
Bug fixes and typo corrections made to this version:	N/a. Indeed this version may well still contain typos and need minor corrections.
Known issues and problems not yet resolved:	See the section in the conclusion on areas for further research.

"The peculiar evil of silencing the expression of an opinion is that it is robbing the human race; posterity as well as the existing generation; those who dissent from the opinion, still more than those who hold it. If the opinion is right, they are deprived of the opportunity of exchanging error for truth: if wrong, they lose, what is almost as great a benefit, the clearer perception and livelier impression of truth, produced by its collision with error."

John Stuart Mill, *On Liberty*, 1869

Chapter 1 - Introduction

Welcome to the incomplete guide to agile marketing. The book that aims to take you on a journey through the world of agile thinking and, no matter how much you may or may not know about agile right now, leave you able to understand why agile is now so important to the field of marketing, and why, when and how to make use of it in your marketing, PR and communications campaigns.

Before I talk more about how this book came to be, I think it's worth explaining why this book is called 'The Incomplete Guide'. Surely you'd be much better buying and reading a complete guide to agile marketing rather than an incomplete one? At the very least, isn't giving it a title like this pretty rubbish marketing on the part of the author?

Well, no. You see, agility is all about adaptation, change and responding to the needs of your customer by constantly maximising the amount of value you give to them. You, dear reader, are my customer, and if I told you this guide were complete, then I'd risk setting it in stone rather than listening to your feedback and constantly adapting, editing and improving the book as a result. In my opinion, any guide to agile marketing that claimed to be complete would only be lying to its readers. As you shall see as you explore this book, any guide to agile marketing can only ever be incomplete, and can only be all the better for being so.

At its heart, this is a book about change. About how digital technologies and the Internet have come along and fundamentally changed the practice of marketing, PR and communication in ways none of us can yet fully understand. It is also a book about how marketers and comms people can use agile thinking to respond to these changes, from the upper levels of strategic thinking right down to the day-to-day practices of delivering marketing campaigns.

From a personal perspective, it is a book that is written by someone who has been on a pretty intense journey of agile discovery over the last 10 years. My first encounter with agile was when I was suddenly handed a copy of a book called 'The Toyota Way' and told I was now a scrum product owner for a piece of software. Little did I understand the differences, nuances and disagreements between these two quite simple things, and I was by and large left to muddle through, I googled what I could, and largely discovered my mistakes through the medium of shouty or passive-aggressive software developers. In essence, I was thrown unexpectedly into the deep end of agile thinking and practice. However, rather than drowning, I taught myself to swim, and I'd like to think that my more than 10 years of learning and practical experience have led to this book now being a pretty solid ship within the world of agile. One we can all use to explore the uncharted territories of digital marketing together.

This book is not just about agile and its associated methodologies though. Over the last two years, I've been lucky enough to spend my evenings and weekends studying for another masters degree at the University of Bristol here in the UK. This degree has been titled 'Strategy, Change and Leadership', basically an MBA without the maths, and through studying for it, I have been struck by one fascinating thing. Whether you read the academic literature on leadership, or strategy, or organisational change, agile thinking is right there in each and every one of them, running like some continuous unifying thread through all three. Now the authors in these specific fields don't often appear to have noticed this. They don't even use the word agile by and large, but the synergies between their ideas and agile thinking are unmistakable. So as much as this book is titled about agile marketing, it is actually a book that looks at how agile applies to leadership, strategy and organisational change as it does to marketing alone. This may seem like a distraction, but to my mind it's absolutely crucial. For if digital and the internet are changing the practice of marketing so fundamentally, we need to take a fundamental look at how marketing is currently led and strategized, and also how we might get the necessary changes to happen.

Another benefit of this book delving so deep into the how and why of marketers adopting an agile mindset is to try to build consensus amongst marketers and prevent their agile transformation being hampered by an issue that has become hugely prevalent in agile transformation within the software industry. You see, in my experience, and in the experience of many others too judging by accounts in the academic literature, agile is a topic that can provoke huge amounts of argument. In some respects it almost feels almost like communism in the 20th century. Like communism, agile is an idea that was intended to help people work together better, but instead provoked endless argument over its meaning and how it should be implemented, with numerous factions splitting and arguing that theirs is 'the one true way'. Whilst I hope no one has ever done a Trotsky and caught an ice axe with their head at a scrum meeting, sometimes the possibility of it doesn't feel entirely remote.

So, if my experiences in agile can help you avoid the same things, and help you get as much benefit out of agile as it promises to deliver, then this book will have served its purpose well. This is not all about me helping you though. This book itself is being written using an agile approach. I fully intend to write it iteratively, releasing as many updates and changes to it on as regular a basis as time and customer feedback will allow. As a result, this book is currently by no means perfect. It identifies as many areas for further research and exploration as it does give solid concrete answers. Some of these areas I will research myself, others will require readers from many different sectors and backgrounds to feed in their questions, queries, errors and bug reports. I'll be equally happy if you absolutely hate this book as if you absolutely love it, as long as in either scenario you get in touch to let me know what you love or hate. Similarly if there's a part of the book that makes no sense to you, be reassured that the fault is with me for not explaining it well enough, not with you for not understanding it. Get in touch, let me know what you're not getting, and I'll look at how I update the explanation for you in a future version of the book. So, whatever you think of this book, either email me your thoughts to gez@bunnypicnic.co.uk, or in the spirit of open data, post them on the Amazon page for the book for me and everyone else to read too.

Whether you love it, hate it or just don't get it, I do hope this book provides you with some food for thought. In relation to the field of agile marketing, the book can best be summed up by a quotation from Winston Churchill:

> "*This is not the end. It is not even the beginning of the end. But it is, perhaps, the end of the beginning.*"

Gez Smith
Bristol, January 2016

Chapter 2 - Why Agility Matters

So why are so many people talking about agile in the fields of marketing, PR and communications? Surely these practices have been around long enough now that we fundamentally know how to do them? After all this time, we must know what works, what doesn't work, and how to deliver the things that work in the most efficient and effective way possible. Well, in many cases this is true, but the thing that's thrown a spanner in the works for communications people across the globe is the Internet. In this chapter, I'd like to look at how the Internet has changed the practice of marketing and communications from a strategic point of view, and how this change requires marketers to question everything they thought they knew about their practice and industry. This is not to say that everything that is questioned will need to be changed. It may be that despite the rise of the Internet, some fundamental truths to marketing and communications remain unaltered. However, with the changes the Internet is bringing about, nothing should be immune from being at least being questioned and examined once more.

So then, what's the one overriding quality of the Internet that makes me think we should question everything we thought we knew about marketing and communications? Fundamentally, from a strategic point of view, it's all about how the Internet is so completely new, both to the world of marketing and even to the world of strategy. Previously, changes in the world around them may have altered the approaches marketers took; the economy moves from growth into recession, your investors turn from bulls into bears. These were big changes no doubt, but they're all things that have happened before, will happen again, and as a result, they have well tested strategies one can adopt in response. The Internet however, hasn't happened before. Sure, it's been around a decent amount of time now, but in terms of mass appeal and widespread usage, you're only looking at around 15 to 20 years maximum.

From a marketing point of view, take a look at when many of the different channels marketers now use were first made available.

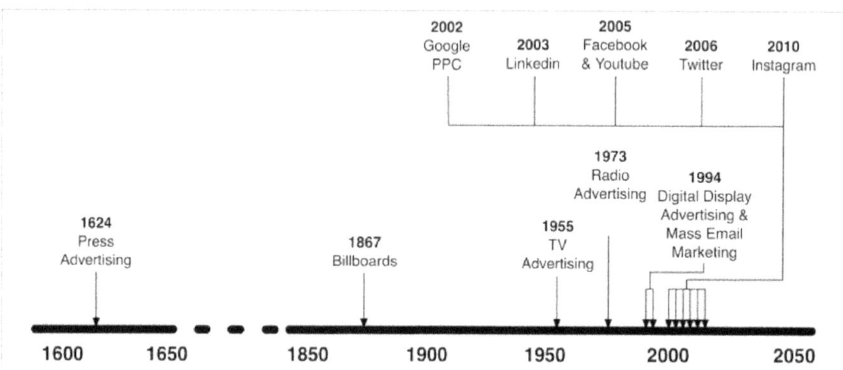

As you can see, the 1900's were not without their changes for marketers. TV advertising will have taken time to get a handle on and optimise, likewise radio advertising too. Although TV and radio were hardly new media by the time either of them introduced advertising. Suddenly however, at the end of the 20th century, a whole plethora of new channels emerged; digital display advertising, email marketing, Pay-Per-Click (PPC) advertising and numerous social media platforms.

Now, you may think I'm cheating a bit here to help my argument. If radio advertising is just one channel, then why are the social media platforms not just one channel as well? Indeed, isn't digital as a whole just a channel, just like radio and TV? Isn't all that has happened just the emergence of one new channel called digital, which is now gamely trying to compete with the serious channels of TV, press and radio? To speak to some in the industry, you may very well believe this to be the case. However, I believe it is views like this that will be forced to evolve or die over the coming years, in ways we can't yet fully understand.

To look more closely at the issue of whether the Internet has led to multiple new channels or just one single channel called digital, let's compare advertising on the photo and video sharing platform Instagram with advertising on the radio. On one level, Instagram is about sharing information in a visual form with others, but then so to some degree are Linkedin and Twitter. Similarly, radio stations are all about sharing information in an audio form with listeners. In terms of the broad types of information shared then, social media channels are not any more or less distinct from one another than radio stations. Equally, if you look at demographics, Instagram users may have different demographic profiles to users of LinkedIn and Twitter, but then so do the listeners of different radio stations.

However, for me, the thing that makes digital platforms into individual channels rather than one collective channel is the format of the information you can share within them. In radio, if you recorded a radio advert, you could in theory run it on any radio station anywhere. A radio ad designed for Classic FM might sound odd if played out on Kiss FM, but you could fundamentally play it. However, if you created an ad for one digital channel, the likelihood is that you just could not run it in the same format on another channel. The tweet you promote on Twitter can only be a maximum of 140 characters, your PPC ad on Google no more than 95 characters, whilst Facebook gives you a massive 420 characters before people have to click 'see more', with a maximum limit of 63,206 characters if you really feel so inclined.

As for images, those on Facebook currently appear at 504px wide, those on Twitter 525px wide, whilst those on Pinterest are just 238px wide, until you expand them, when they become 736px wide[1] . Even worse, if you want to put an image on Instagram, it has to be square, 640px by 640px, but if you want to put an image on your Google PPC ad, you can't. Up until 2014, you could put images on organic Google results, and wise practitioners were encouraging people to do so, until Google removed this functionality

---

1 http://www.adweek.com/socialtimes/ultimate-social-network-cheat-sheet/613044

completely. On top of this, there are numerous other small differences between channels, such as the speed that content flows through them, the differences in how they make their content publicly available or only viewable by logged in and interconnected users, even the different ways they allow hashtags to function.

In short, the Internet is like a modern day Babel, every channel having its own unique nature and requirements, meaning they cannot be approached in a single and collective manner in the way traditional marketing channels could be. Even if two channels do share common functionality for a time, as events like Google's removal of images from organic search results shows, it is likely that such commonalities may later suddenly change. As a result, I believe digital is not a channel. Indeed, it is a word that covers such a vast, varied and complex menagerie of different marketing and communication channels that it is rapidly becoming so broad as to be meaningless.

So then, the Internet has brought about a huge range of new channels for marketers to get to grips with, each with their own nuances and technical requirements. However, there is also another fundamental change the Internet has brought about in the field of marketing, namely the unpredictability of the consumer environment when receiving marketing communications. Previously, if you put advertising on a billboard, you knew that the people who saw it would necessarily be in the vicinity of the billboard. If you put an advertisement on the TV, you may not have known exactly what environment those people were in, but you knew they were most likely sitting down, probably in their living room at home, and most certainly watching TV. However, digital has not just introduced new channels and media, it's also introduced new environments. With the massive rise of mobile enabled smart phones, people consuming your marketing could still be in their living room at home or on the bus near a billboard, but they could equally well be in the pub, walking in the countryside or on the toilet.

Not only this, but the Internet has even reshaped traditional channels such as TV. Originally, you knew when people saw your adverts, as you had a list of the spot times setting out what time the ads would be broadcast. With the advent of the VCR, this changed slightly, as there was now a chance people were watching your ad at some other time, but in practice this was likely to be a relatively small and insignificant development. Most people who saw your ads saw them at the times you had them broadcast. Now though, with the widespread prevalence of HD recorders and many channels offering a '+1' service as standard, coupled with the massive proliferation in the number of channels available[2], the likelihood is that people will be watching your ads at all manner of times. That is, if they're watching them at all. Everyone I know who watches TV that they've set a reminder to record, or who watches catch up TV generally, fast forwards or otherwise skips the commercial breaks. Not only this, but it's possible they're now not really watching TV at all. With the concept of 'second screening' alarming marketers across the globe, it could be that your audience is now watching TV, reading Twitter, posting on Facebook and chatting face to face to people in the room all at the same time. In short, thanks to the rise of the Internet, even good old TV advertising isn't the same as it used to be.

The Internet has also changed another crucial component of successful marketing, the component of data. We shall return to this aspect later in this book, but digital marketing has access to a hugely increased range of data compared with traditional marketing such as press, radio and TV. Not only is the range of data increased, so is its volume, its detail and its speed. In the UK,

---

[2] At least in the UK. I know the USA has been God's country in this regard for far longer than us backward Brits.

BARB TV ratings started in 1981 with 3,000 homes in its panel[3], a methodological approach that took some time to report back to the marketers who were interested in it. Now in 2015, you could show tens of thousands of people a video on Facebook in just a few hours, collect accurate data on multiple aspects of each and every viewer individually, and do this all in real time.

Looking further at the detail of data digital marketing allows you to capture, it isn't just that you can now know more about the age, gender, location and interests of the people consuming your marketing. Of course you can, and this is immensely useful. However, the more fundamental change is the fact that in digital marketing, your consumers now have so many more options for talking back to you too. As your TV ad plays, you can read the responses people are tweeting about it in real time. If you get complaints from customers, you can see all of those on various social media channels too. Indeed, you can even go whole hog and start having regular conversations with your customers online, and watch them have conversations about your brand with others too. In the old days, when you put a TV ad out, people watched it and maybe discussed it with people they knew. Nowadays, people may watch it, discuss it with people they know, discuss it with people they don't know, leave comments about it online that can still be read years later, even create and distribute their own parodies of it online. The Internet and digital are changing marketing from a situation where marketers push messages at consumers, to one where the relationship between them could easily become a meaningful, constant, two-way conversation, carried out in real time.

This leads us back to the issue of speed. Because the Internet lets you publish marketing material much more quickly, and lets you see how it's performing much more quickly too, marketers often

[3] http://www.barb.co.uk/resources/tv-facts/tv-since-1981/1981

feel that they need to be able to do their work more quickly in order to keep up. The example of Oreo Cookies getting a 'real-time' response out on Twitter to the power cut during Superbowl XLVII in 2013[4] has been cited to death ever since, but the thing that captures the attention of marketers is not the response Oreos put out, but the fact they could put it out for mass consumption within minutes at all.

Previously, if the only channels marketers had to use were TV, press and radio, then the speed at which you could get a response out to an event was necessarily limited by the speed with which those channels could schedule your message in. Press was likely to be the fastest of these channels, but even then you had to wait until the next day's print run at the earliest. Now, digital channels let you set your message live as soon as you have created it, and your biggest limiting factor in terms of speed has become your organisation and its internal marketing processes.

As a result, we get one of the biggest misunderstandings in the field of agile marketing at the moment, that idea that being more agile is just about being more speedy and responsive. Sadly, it isn't. We shall examine this in some more detail later, but for now, just remember that saying agility is the same as speed is like saying jogging is the same as being thin. Jogging can lead to being thin, and agile can certainly lead to massive speed to market improvements. However, it is perfectly possible to be a fat jogger, and it is just as possible to be a slow agile practitioner.

We can see then that talk of the Internet 'fundamentally changing marketing' is one of the few statements you find online that isn't complete nonsense. It has caused a proliferation in channels, in consumer environments, in audience data and in speed to market,

---

[4] http://www.wired.com/2013/02/oreo-twitter-super-bowl/ See the original here https://twitter.com/oreo/status/298246571718483968

all over a relatively short space of time. This all adds up to one fundamental truth.

The Internet has changed so many variables that we cannot yet be certain what the best approach is when using it for marketing.

Of course, we can find this out. Indeed, I suspect in time, thanks to the proliferation of data in digital marketing, we will actually have a better handle on how it works and how to optimise it than for any channel we've previously used. However, right now, only around 10 years since these huge changes in channels, environments, data and speed have first arisen, we just can't know for certain.

So what does this mean for marketing strategy?

First, it explains why the Internet is currently so full of meaningless hyperbole about digital marketing. Marketers who have previously been able to sound so confident about the marketing they create, and with good reason, are now left floundering. Rather than admit to a lack of knowledge at such a late (and very often senior) stage in their careers, they use digital buzzwords in the hope no one will call their bluff and ask for a definition. Very often it works, but I would argue strongly that it really shouldn't. Faced with such a new and complex environment as the Internet, we all need to get to grips with it very quickly, even if this means looking clueless in the short term.

My reason for making this point is that agile is one of the most abused words in digital marketing right now. As we have already seen, people conflate it with speed to market, reduced bureaucracy and all manner of other good things. We shall return to this problem in the next chapter, but first we must consider another word that's still abused far more than the word agile ever is. That word is strategy.

I'm always surprised by just how popular the word strategy is online, and especially in the world of digital marketing. In this brave new digital world, strategy is everything. For example, in the last year, how often have you heard people say that you need a social media strategy? Now, compare that with how often you have heard people say you need a social media plan. For some reason, the words 'social media' have become inextricably linked with the word strategy. At the time of writing, a search on Google for 'social media strategy' returns over 5 million results, a search for 'social media plan' just over 500,000.

However, how many people actually know what they mean by the word strategy? I'd wager many do not, and just use it because it makes them sound authoritative. In a digital world that's become more complex and less certain, saying you're a digital strategist applies a comforting veneer of competence and certainty to things that you know deep down you don't fully understand. In reality, strategy is a hugely contested term, and the only people who can rightfully claim to understand what it means are those who admit their definition may be theirs alone. As Carter, Clegg and Kornberger note:

> *"There are almost as many definitions of strategy as there are strategists."* [5]

So if marketers are to get to grips with this changed digital world, then part of this understanding may come from understanding what is meant by strategy. We might not yet fully understand how marketing works on the Internet, and there aren't many marketing precedents to turn to for help, but there are definitely precedents we can learn from in the broader world of strategic thinking. If the Internet is making the environment of the marketer uncertain and

---

[5] Carter, C.,Clegg, S.R., & Kornberger, M. (2010). *A very short, fairly interesting and reasonably cheap book about studying strategy*. London: Sage. p. 8.

unknown, then it is to the world of strategy that we should turn our attention. For the academic field of strategy has been looking at how to respond to complex and uncertain environments for years and has, I believe, a great deal to teach us about how to respond to the uncertainties the Internet is creating for marketers.

One potentially useful strategic model relating to the external environment is the 'Five Forces' model developed by a chap called Michael Porter. In this model, Porter details five forces in the external environment of a business which influence the formulation of its strategy. These are its competitors, customers, suppliers, potential entrants and substitutes, which, for the purposes of this model, are each broken down into smaller elements[6].

Just a glance through some of the component elements of each force highlights the significant strategic problems marketers face in the field of digital marketing. According to Porter, one strategic advantage a company can have exists when buyers face significant switching costs, meaning that they are less likely to move to a rival supplier. In the Internet marketplace, switching from one supplier to another has now become as simple clicking a few buttons. Porter also states that markets are strategically less attractive when competitors are numerous and roughly equal in size and power. The Internet has massively increased this problem for marketers. TV advertising used to be the preserve of the larger organisations with budget to pay for it. Now even a new entrant to a market can film a high quality advertisement on their iPhone, edit it on their computer, upload it to Youtube and share it through social media for minimal monetary or opportunity cost. Of course,

---

[6] Porter, M. E. (2008). 'The five competitive forces that shape strategy', *Harvard Business Review*, Vol. 86, No. 1, pp. 78-93.

money still matters, large advertisers can pay to reach wider audiences online through financial investment, but the marketplace has nonetheless been significantly leveled.

As a result, from an external perspective, Eisenhardt and Sull have hit the nail on the head by stating:

> *"The Internet portal space is a strategist's worst nightmare: it's characterised by intense rivalries, instant imitators, and customers who refuse to pay a cent. Worse yet, there are few barriers to entry."* [7]

So from an external perspective, Porter's model for strategy seems to confirm what we have already discussed about the impact of the Internet on the world of marketing. It has made it far more complex, fast-paced and uncertain. But what use is strategy if it only confirms what you already know, that the Internet and digital technologies have significantly disrupted marketing in many ways? Whilst confirmation of our problem may be reassuring, what we really need is strategic thinking that tells us what to do in this new complex and uncertain marketing environment.

To start to find this, let's look at those strategic theories that focus more on the internal elements of an organisation and its strategy formulation. One key school in this field is called the Resource Based View. In simple terms, this model looks at strategy in terms of the resources and capabilities an organisation has for operating in a given marketplace. How should organisational resources and capabilities inform the strategic response to the uncertainty digital marketing creates? First, there is obviously the point

[7] Eisenhardt, K.M., & Sull, D.N. (2001). 'Strategy as simple rules', *Harvard Business Review*, Vol. 79, No. 1, p. 108.

we have touched upon above. If you are to align your marketing resources into capabilities in this changed digital world, you have to be aware that your old capabilities may not fit the changed environment. This sounds obvious, but there are still many huge marketing departments and award winning agencies that have yet to understand the true nature and scale of the change digital will require, and so continue to employ their standard marketing approaches in a digital world.

After all, Youtube's a good place to put your TV ads right? Aren't display ads just a shorter and more simple version of a TV ad too? Come to think of it, tweets are pretty much the same length as the copy on some of your billboard posters. These beliefs may potentially be true, but unless we stop and truly reflect on how digital might alter current marketing approaches, we're very much at risk of them not being true but following them anyway.

The Internet also provides another interesting challenge to how you align your marketing resources. Often, a broader strategic approach to marketing sees the target audience purely as the final end consumer of what is produced. For traditional marketing, such as TV, radio and billboards, this is largely accurate. However, Internet channels allow your advertising to be shared by those who consume it, giving you access to the consumer's audiences, and gaining credibility for your messages via social proofing. As such, consumers are here performing the same role as the people who develop and distribute traditional marketing content. More than ever before, and for better or worse, your customers are now doing your marketing for you. They have in many ways become your media suppliers, only you can't control them or pay them to do what you want.

Of course, this has to some degree been true since the dawn of marketing itself. Someone buy your product or sees your marketing. They like it and so share information about it with other people through word of mouth. However, the Internet has vastly increased the scale of the phenomenon, and the fidelity of it too. Word of mouth advertising is necessarily limited in scale by how many people any one individual can speak to. Equally, as the people they speak to pass the message on to others, the message is prone to the concept of Chinese whispers[8], meaning what is said about you may be different from the message you hoped would be shared. On the Internet, for example through a retweet, people can share your marketing with hundreds, even thousands of people with just the click of a button, and more important, share it without changing it one iota. Thus from a strategic alignment point of view, the Internet has flipped the 'marketer / consumer' relationship on its head. Your consumers are now also your fellow marketers, and you've lost a lot of control over where your marketing ends up.

So Porter's idea of strategy has confirmed to us that the Internet creates a problem for traditional marketers, and applying the Resource Based View gives us a much greater understanding of the sorts of things may have changed in the world of digital marketing, but we still need to go down another level. What sort of strategy can marketers use day to day in adapting to and coping with this change and complexity? For me, the answer to this lies in the academic idea of strategy being either deliberate or emergent. A deliberate strategy is set before implementation, detailed to a high degree, followed unwaveringly and delivered exactly as planned, achieving its intended results[9]. As such, to me it

[8] http://en.wikipedia.org/wiki/Chinese_whispers

sounds uncannily like traditional approaches to marketing, with its legion of marketing planners, detailed pre-campaign specification of channels and spend, and the up-front creation of all of its marketing assets before the campaign goes live.

In contrast, an emergent strategy grows in the absence of intention towards any given forms of action, and is more adaptive to external forces. Of course, both forms of strategy are unlikely to exist in their purest form. Purely deliberate strategy would be entirely unaffected by external forces; purely emergent strategy would require an absence of intention toward forms of action. Thus most strategies sit somewhere on a continuum between the two.

As I just mentioned, I would argue that in most traditional marketing, the process is much more on the deliberate end of the scale, constrained by the need to manage a large and complex campaign. This approach is entirely understandable, given that until the rise of the Internet, the commercial marketing environment was relatively mature, stable and predictable. Fashions came and went, successes occasionally came from left-field, but you knew that delivering marketing was your organisation's job, you knew which channels you'd use, you knew how best to use them, you knew where your consumers were likely to be when consuming your marketing, and you knew how and when you'd find out if any of it had worked. You could thus use deliberate strategy for marketing, planning your campaign, specifying the assets and channels, follow the plan from start to finish and quite often arrive at the end goal you expected.

---

[9] Mintzberg, H., & Waters, J.A. (1985). 'Of strategies, deliberate and emergent', *Strategic Management Journal*, Vol. 6, No. 3, pp. 257-272.

However, as we have seen, the digital environment currently contains very few of these certainties. People are finding out answers to them every day for sure, but there are still too many unknowns to be certain of much at all, and new developments are creating new uncertainties the whole time. This is where we start to find a clear route to solving the problems of complexity and uncertainty caused by the rise of digital and the Internet. Mintzberg, one of the key thinkers in the field of deliberate and emergent strategy, suggests the answer lies in matching the strategy you take to the environment in which you operate. Complex and rapidly changing environments require you to follow emergent strategies, whilst simple, stable and well-understood environments are best suited by deliberate strategies.

So if the environment in which marketers used to operate was indeed simple, stable and well-understood, then you can see why marketing and communications as a practice has got into the habit of following a strategically deliberate approach. After all, where else is this writ larger than the fact that being a 'planner' is a specific type of marketing job with its own well-trodden career path? Sadly, it is exactly this industry approach that is so challenged by the rise of the Internet and digital marketing.

Whilst some have noticed this already, many more have not. Indeed, I suspect what is very often happening at the moment is that traditional marketers, used to formulating deliberate marketing strategies and employing tried and tested campaign delivery approaches, are being left flummoxed by the unknowns of the digital space. Lacking the strategic tools to make sense of this, all they can do is redouble their efforts in making ever more deliberate strategies, seeking confidence and security in their familiar territories, and compounding their problem in the process. The more the old deliberate approaches fail to work, the more people work harder and harder at following them, convinced that with enough planning, enough best practice and an extremely detailed campaign delivery schedule to stick to religiously, the challenges of marketing to and communicating with people online can be cracked.

Unfortunately, I believe this approach is doomed to failure, which is why I wanted to explain to you first the strategic issues around digital marketing. As if you don't understand these, the risk is you'll quickly fall back into your old deliberate habits and start falling behind competitors that do understand the changes the Internet has brought about. So if an emergent strategy is the right one to follow in the complex and uncertain digital environment, then what exactly would that entail doing? How do you apply an emergent strategy approach to your digital marketing?

Well, this is where agile comes in.

Chapter 3 - What Is Agile?

If you don't know what agile is at all right now, don't worry. If you still don't get it at the end of this section, don't worry either. As we work through the concepts and discussion in this book, you'll start to understand how agile is a philosophy, a mindset, a way of seeing the world and approaching your work based on some very simple, and enjoyable, principles. It's also a very contested term, one that gives the impression of being far more settled and agreed upon than it actually is.

Agile as a widespread concept was born out of a document called the agile manifesto. The history of how the manifesto came about is all written up at http://agilemanifesto.org, but in case you've not got time to have a read at the moment, it happened like this.

"*On February 11-13, 2001, at The Lodge at Snowbird ski resort in the Wasatch mountains of Utah, seventeen people met to talk, ski, relax, and try to find common ground and of course, to eat. What emerged was the agile Software Development Manifesto. Representatives from Extreme Programming, SCRUM, DSDM, Adaptive Software Development, Crystal, Feature-Driven Development, Pragmatic Programming, and others sympathetic to the need for an alternative to documentation driven, heavyweight software development processes convened* [10]"

As you read that, you may notice one significant issue. This agile manifesto is all about developing software. Indeed, in the above source, it's not technically called the agile manifesto, it's actually called the 'agile Software Development Manifesto'. So unless they were delivering software as part of a marketing campaigns, why on earth would a marketer want to sign up to this manifesto? Well, that's what this book's here to explore, but for me, the first reason

[10] Taken from http://agilemanifesto.org/history.html

marketers should want to follow this manifesto is that whilst it was created with software development in mind, it's actually something much broader.

The agile manifesto is a mindset and an approach to work that has the potential to be transferred across many different areas of life. After all, if traditional project management approaches such as PRINCE2 can be used in many different industries, why can't agile be too? To understand this a little better, let's have a look at what the agile manifesto actually recommends.

Over the course of those few days at that ski resort in Utah, the 17 originators of the agile manifesto came up with the following [11].

"*We are uncovering better ways of developing software by doing it and helping others do it.*

Through this work we have come to value:

- ***Individuals and interactions*** *over* ***processes and tools***
- ***Working software*** *over* ***comprehensive documentation***
- ***Customer collaboration*** *over* ***contract negotiation***
- ***Responding to change*** *over* ***following a plan***

That is, while there is value in the items on the right, we value the items on the left more."

Now this is an interesting approach to defining how work should be carried out, as it doesn't really deal in absolutes. It doesn't say 'thou shalt do this' and 'thou shalt not do that', but instead talks about which behaviours agile practitioners value more than other behaviours. It is all about shades of grey rather than black and white, and I suspect this is one of the many reasons why agile is

[11] Taken from www.agilemanifesto.org

such a misunderstood, contested and fiercely argued over term. It's also why agile is much more a mindset or philosophy than a strict process to be followed. What you value is a function of how your mind is arranged. No one but you can control exactly how much you value something. The other interesting thing to note here is that the manifesto itself actually only mentions software once, in its opening line. So try this. Re-read the above manifesto now, but replace the words 'developing software' with 'developing marketing campaigns'. Does the whole thing still make sense? Absolutely it does. So I'd call that the first test passed as to whether the agile manifesto might be able to be transferred from the world of software development into the world of marketing.

The agile manifesto isn't entirely the whole story though. Sitting beneath it are 12 principles which agile practitioners should follow [12].

"Our highest priority is to satisfy the customer through early and continuous delivery of valuable software.

Welcome changing requirements, even late in development. Agile processes harness change for the customer's competitive advantage.

Deliver working software frequently, from a couple of weeks to a couple of months, with a preference to the shorter timescale.

Business people and developers must work together daily throughout the project.

Build projects around motivated individuals. Give them the environment and support they need, and trust them to get the job done.

[12] Taken from www.agilemanifesto.org/principles.html

The most efficient and effective method of conveying information to and within a development team is face-to-face conversation.

Working software is the primary measure of progress.

Agile processes promote sustainable development. The sponsors, developers, and users should be able to maintain a constant pace indefinitely.

Continuous attention to technical excellence and good design enhances agility.

Simplicity--the art of maximizing the amount of work not done--is essential.

The best architectures, requirements, and designs emerge from self-organizing teams.

At regular intervals, the team reflects on how to become more effective, then tunes and adjusts its behavior accordingly."

Now these principles are a little more directive than the manifesto itself, showing how the manifesto comes to life in various different scenarios, and giving practitioners some goals to work towards in their practice. That said, many of these principles are themselves very much mindsets rather than actions to take or processes to follow. The principle;

"Welcome changing requirements, even late in development"

absolutely has to be a mindset rather than a process. Imagine the last time someone got in touch with you to say they wanted to change some important component of your marketing campaign a few days before the campaign was due to launch. Did you welcome that change, or did you rage at a co-worker about it before flying into a blind panic?

Personally, I do now more often than not welcome change, and I have to say it's immensely liberating once you do, but it's no easy thing to do, and I'm sure I'm still guilty of not exactly welcoming it from time to time. Similarly;

> *"Simplicity - the art of maximising the amount of work not done"*

is a simple thing to say, but again it's a mindset and an approach rather than a process or action. How far do you maximise it? Are there any instances when you should not? None of this is answered by the manifesto, for as it says, maximising the amount of work not done is an art, not a science.

Now this is all very well, but how does the busy marketing practitioner make use of all of this? As we'll consider throughout this book, we're all used to following processes, to planning, to setting budgets, to hitting delivery dates, to measuring progress and all sorts of other much more clear, black and white approaches to marketing. Agile being a philosophy and a mindset is all well and good, but we haven't all got time to spend sitting cross-legged listening to Brian Eno in a fog of incense just to change our worldview. If agile's going to take off in the world of marketing, it needs to have at least a few concrete things people should start doing, and things they should stop doing. Besides, whilst the points in the manifesto are all well and good, aren't they also a bit obvious? We all know we should collaborate more, keep things more simple, trust those around us, and reflect on how to become more efficient. Isn't this manifesto just a collection of truisms and statements of the obvious? In short, isn't it all just a load of tree hugging hippie crap?

Well, I would argue no, for two very good reasons. First, if you find yourself thinking that it's tree hugging hippie crap, then the manifesto has clearly touched a nerve with you. You may know you should collaborate more and keep things more simple, but if you're honest with yourself, how much do you really do this day to day? How often do you actually keep information or ideas to yourself in case someone else takes the credit, or messes them up? How often do you find yourself sighing 'If you want a job done properly, do it yourself'?

This is not to say that acting in this way is your fault. Often it's what you do because it seems to be the safest, easiest or most rational thing to do in the environment in which you're operating. Agile needs evangelists in the world of marketing and communications, but it doesn't need martyrs. If you rush straight to an agile approach in an otherwise massively un-agile environment, you may come a cropper pretty quickly. So through all of this, don't just assume that you're always living the agile values, or that others around you truly are either. Being agile takes work, and the road to hell is paved with good intentions.

Second, the world of agile does in fact have some processes and procedures you can follow; some ways to show that you're working with agile; some day to day practices you can do to help learn and embed the agile mindset in your grey matter until it becomes second nature. If you look back at the first excerpt from the agile manifesto at the start of this chapter, you'll see it says that that 2001 meeting in Utah featured:

> "*Representatives from Extreme Programming, SCRUM, DSDM, Adaptive Software Development, Crystal, Feature-Driven Development, Pragmatic Programming*".

All of these are software development methodologies, practices people use to design, build, test, release and refine software programs. They are also practices that existed before the agile manifesto was agreed. As a result, the manifesto was always bound to be a philosophy, as it needed to become the connecting thread through a number of different process-based methodologies. Now when you get into the area of methodologies, agile as it currently stands become a little more problematic to move over into the world of marketing. As you might expect, some of the practices within the methodologies initially seem specific to building software, and we shall return to look at examples of these in more detail later in the book.

This is though an area that's not been well enough thought through in the field of agile marketing and communications; the degree to which the different agile software development methodologies can and cannot be translated across from one field to the other. This is most likely to due the very simple fact that an advanced software developer or practitioner is very unlikely to quit their field and make the move over to become a marketing campaign manager. A lot of the agile knowledge is currently locked up in the agile software community, and it will take time to uncover and translate it across into marketing activity.

One common habit you do see though, and one I myself have followed, is to start with a methodology for implementing agile called scrum. Scrum is, or at least should be, simple, and it looks most like the sort of project management methodology that we're all used to working with, with set meetings, set formats for meetings, regular check ins on the progress of the work and all those other comfort blankets we have been brought clinging to. This book will look at scrum as the approach to delivering agile in an organisation, but only as an initial step. There is much work yet to be done to look at how the other agile methodologies may work in the context of marketing and communications, and potentially much value to be gained from doing so.

Before we disappear any further down the rabbit hole, let us take a step back and consider everything we've just learned about agile in the context of the previous chapter. Our problem is that we need to find a strategic approach that matches the complexity, uncertainty and speed of change found in the digital marketing and communications environment. In this regard, agile is potentially a very good fit. It doesn't do away with some of the practices of old, such as process, tools and planning, but it de-prioritises them in favour of responding to change, constantly putting things out there to see how they work, and focusing on simplicity in order to make progress. As a result, it doesn't bet the organisation's future on one particular approach, and so reduces the risk of moving into new territories. A move to an agile approach changes the emphasis of your activity from big up-front planning to making numerous decisions during the process of execution. Through this, your plan emerges, perhaps even to the point that you will only know what your plan was once your project has ended. Now whilst all of this is true for agile, could it not also be said to be true of a number of different approaches too?

One of the things I notice a lot in discussing agile with people is how confusing the conversation can be, even before you get into the issue of how to translate it from software development into marketing. You see, agile is very similar to a lot of other thinking in the field of project management, and as a result is sometimes very hard to disentangle from other approaches. Indeed, I'm often not convinced there's a huge amount of point in doing so. For example, one thing agile practitioners try to do is differentiate agile from what is called a lean approach. Lean as an approach started in the world of manufacturing, but was translated across into software development by Mary and Tom Poppendieck, and has seven principles.

"1. Eliminate Waste
2. Build Quality In
3. Create Knowledge
4. Defer Commitment
5. Deliver Fast
6. Respect People
7. Optimize the Whole[13]"

Now if you think back to the agile manifesto, you can see some immediate synergies between it and lean. The lean principle of 'eliminate waste' is very similar to the agile principle of 'maximising the amount of work not done'. Likewise, 'respect people' is similar to agile's 'trust them to get the job done'. Equally, lean's 'deliver fast' is just like agile's 'deliver working software frequently, from a couple of weeks to a couple of months, with a preference to the shorter timescale'. Lean's 'optimise the whole' is like agile's 'at regular intervals, the team reflects on how to become more effective, then tunes and adjusts its behavior accordingly'. You get the idea. A big irony with arguments about whether agile is lean, or lean is agile, or neither of them are either of the other, is not only that they're likely to be the sort of waste of effort that both of them would argue against, but also that lean itself is often confused with the methodology from which it originated, called the Toyota Way.

Now, this Toyota Way approach has fourteen principles[14], which read as follows.

"Base your management decisions on a long-term philosophy, even at the expense of short-term financial goals.

---

[13] Poppendieck, M., & Poppendieck, T. (2009). *Leading lean software development: Results are not the point,* Upper Saddle River, NJ: Addison-Wesley. See also http://www.hackerchick.com/2012/01/agile-vs-lean-yeah-yeah-whats-the-difference.html

[14] Liker, J. K. (2004). *The Toyota Way*, New York: McGraw-Hill

Create a continuous process flow to bring problems to the surface.

Use 'pull' systems to avoid overproduction.

Level out the workload (work like the tortoise, not the hare).

Build a culture of stopping to fix problems, to get quality right the first time.

Standardized tasks and processes are the foundation for continuous improvement and employee empowerment.

Use visual controls so no problems are hidden.

Use only reliable, thoroughly tested technology that serves your people and process.

Grow leaders who thoroughly understand the work, live the philosophy, and teach it to others.

Develop exceptional people and teams who follow your company's philosophy.

Respect your extended network of partners and suppliers by challenging them and helping them improve.

Go and see for yourself to thoroughly understand the situation.

Make decisions slowly by consensus, thoroughly considering all options; implement decisions rapidly.

Become a learning organization through relentless reflection and continuous improvement."

The Toyota Way clearly has some differences with agile, although I think these are more in terms of the Toyota Way specifying things the agile manifesto does not, as opposed to any of Toyota actively conflicting or disagreeing with agile. Indeed, Toyota principle number four 'Level out the workload (work like the tortoise not the hare)' is very similar to agile principle number eight, 'agile processes promote sustainable development. The sponsors, developers, and users should be able to maintain a constant pace indefinitely'. We'll return to this idea later, but it is worth noting that a common feature of the scrum process is a scrum board, which is often very functionally similar to the Kanban board Toyota principle number seven would recommend ('Use visual controls so no problems are hidden'). Toyota principle 12, 'Go and see for yourself to thoroughly understand the situation' is not a million miles from agile principle six; 'The most efficient and effective method of conveying information to and within a development team is face-to-face conversation'.

So then, through all of this one thing seems clear. There are potentially lots of interesting ideas in amongst the difference between agile as a philosophy, the different methodologies that people can use to work with agile, and the methodologies similar to agile such as Lean, Kanban and Toyota. However, none of this means that we need to spend a long time vehemently arguing about the minute intricacies of these differences, or thinking that these different approaches fundamentally conflict with one another. Instead, the thing that is worth spending some time examining is the risks these arguments and conflicts can bring to an organisation's or a team's agility. For if we were assessing them using a traditional project management methodology, we'd classify these risks as both high likelihood and high impact.

To avoid these conflicts, we must at all times bear in mind that agile is based on shades of grey, and as such is actually a very hard concept to pin down. As Kruchten says;

"*Agility is not a technology, science, or product but a culture...this presents an even more difficult task: defining culture.*" [15]

For me, agile is one of those things you understand through doing it, living it and experiencing it. Sure, you can learn the principles and use the methodologies, but unless you're truly changing your mindset and the mindset of those working with and around you, then all of this can just be so much window dressing. This of course makes implementing agile into your marketing and communication practices all the harder. You can teach people what agile is in theory, but for it to work, you need to coach them into doing it. You need, literally, to change their minds.

I think the fact that agile is much more a cultural rather than a physical or process change is one of the main reasons it causes people to argue. This is not because arguing is inherent in the nature of agile, or is a requirement in the agile manifesto. Quite the opposite. Agile is all about collaboration, open and frequent communication, and a willingness to change direction as new knowledge emerges, even a willingness to fail and / or be proven wrong. However, because it is a philosophical and cultural change that can be so hard to define, arguments about what agile is and is not are unfortunately sometimes long and vehement. Indeed, Williams and Cockburn suggest that you can trace the roots of agile in the field of software development back to the 1960's, and that the only things that are new about agile as it is currently conceived is;

"*The bundling of the techniques into a theoretical and practical framework and the strong, sometimes vehement, declaration of their importance.*" [16]

---

[15] Kruchten, P. (2007). 'Voyage in the agile memeplex', *ACM Queue*, Vol. 5, No. 5, p. 40.

[16] Cockburn, A., & Williams, L. (2003). 'Agile software development: it's about feedback and change', *Computer*, Vol. 36, No. 6, p. 40.

Kruchten goes further, stating;

> "*I have been distraught at the level of dogmatism, bigotry, contempt, or just plain ignorance that I witness in the agile world.*" [17]

Sadly, based on my experiences of the last 10 years, I have to agree.

It is interesting though that Kruchten notes 'ignorance' as one of the unfortunate features of the agile world, as I think this is a fact too often overlooked. First, it is clear that you don't need a whole lot of knowledge or experience to become a certified practitioner in the field of agile. Often gaining one of the many formal certifications in agile methodologies is as simple as attending a two day course then scoring reasonably highly on a multiple choice test at the end.

However, as I've touched on above, how much could formal training and an exam make you agile anyway, if it is all about cultural and mindset change? I'm certain both training and examinations can help, and neither should be ignored, but they are far from being the only requirements to becoming agile. Indeed, I think it is both significant and excellent that the Scrum Alliance, one of the bodies awarding the Certified Scrum Master qualification, also offer one specific type of certification called Certified Scrum Professional, which you can only gain if you can prove to them directly that you have spent a good amount of time going out and talking to, learning from, even debating with other scrum practitioners about the practice. No exams, no simple tests to pass, just a lot of hard work over a long period of time, and the ability to demonstrate to a real human being that you know what you're talking about when it comes to scrum.

---

[17] Kruchten, P. (2007). 'Voyage in the agile memeplex', *ACM Queue*, Vol. 5, No. 5, p44.

So overall then, agile approaches find themselves with a unique problem. Being a cultural and mindset change, they find it very hard to define themselves exactly. This then makes agile harder to teach to people in the traditional sense, both because teaching someone a new mindset is harder than teaching them a factual process, and because how can you pin down what exactly to teach them anyway? Not only this, but item two of the agile Manifesto openly de-prioritises documenting how agile work is done in favour of producing working outputs. Now item two is one I firmly believe in. Documentation often only adds overhead rather than value to a project, and if I'm asked to choose between lots of documentation and lots of working outputs that I can use in my marketing and communications, I'll always choose the outputs.

However, how do you make the teaching of agile widespread if there is little documentation on it to share? As Kruchten notes;

> "*Much of (agile) is really transmitted by oral tradition and by imitation.*" [18]

This in turn makes it much more prone to argument. Agile is a religion that has no set text, no Bible, no Torah, no Sri Guru Granth Sahib. Indeed, it would probably see having one as a bit on an overhead that took time away from more important work. Thus its followers have nowhere to turn to look for the ultimate truth.

As a result, it is worth stating here that I fully expect people to argue with this book, possibly a lot. It's why I've deliberately put the quote I have from John Stuart Mill at its very start. However, for me, if agile is a mindset, then a lot of this will be about how I choose to frame those arguments in my own mind. If I become

[18] Kruchten, P. (2007). 'Voyage in the agile memeplex', *ACM Queue*, Vol. 5, No. 5, pp. 38-44. p. 40.

defensive against them and argumentative in return, then I won't be embracing the agile technique myself. What one person sees as an attack, another could see as feedback requiring a change, and as principle two of the agile manifesto states, I ought to:

"Welcome changing requirements, even late in development".

So as you consider entering the world of agile, I would caution you not too worry too much about those who argue vehemently, aggressively or angrily over its finer details and its differences between Lean, Kanban, Toyota or anything else. Agile is an indistinct concept that's hard to define exactly. It has few official guiding documents, is hard to teach formally, and is mostly passed down through word of mouth. As a result, it is necessarily shaped and changed over time by the biases and communication abilities of others. Besides, arguing about 'Doing agile Right' is to my mind one of the most ironic arguments you can have. Agile is all about responding to change, being adaptive, collaborating and learning together. Agile arguments further none of these causes, and are best left to those who seem to prefer arguing instead of maximising the amount of work not done. Of all the types of work not to do, arguing is surely one of the most significant. By all means debate, discuss and collaborate over definitions of agile, but heated argument and productive collaboration rarely complement each other.

So we've now looked at the concept of agile from a lot of different perspectives. But before we move on to look at how all of this differs from traditional 'big idea' approaches to marketing, there are two more areas I want to look at first. The first one is hugely important, and is perhaps more important in the world of marketing than it is in the world of software development. As for some reason, a huge amount of the debate around agile marketing at the moment centres around the issue of speed. Somehow, agile marketers, PR or comms people are believed to work more quickly, deliver their campaigns more quickly, even react more quickly to breaking trends, conversations and events online. For all the hype about how agile is about speed, you'd think agile marketers spent their days rushing around doing nothing but delivering outputs as quickly as possible[19].

Of course, the fascinating thing is that agile doesn't actually mean any of this. Think back to the agile manifesto and its principles. Individually, there are lots of things in there that probably do help people work more quickly. Doing the simplest thing possible is bound to be quicker than doing the most complex thing possible. Regularly reflecting on how to become more efficient will probably help with speed too. But nowhere in the manifesto does it say agile makes people much work more quickly. The closest you get to this idea is principle three, which states:

> *"Deliver working software frequently, from a couple of weeks to a couple of months, with a preference to the shorter timescale."*

But this is about delivering working outputs frequently, rather than delivering the whole project more quickly. If you deliver more frequently but also make your outputs smaller, then you'll still be delivering the same amount of work in the same amount of time. You'll just deliver it incrementally rather than in one big bang.

If anything, the agile manifesto actually recommends against working too speedily, principle number eight stating:

> "*Agile processes promote sustainable development. The sponsors, developers, and users should be able to maintain a constant pace indefinitely*".

[19] Incidentally, I can't just blame marketers for that belief. Once when I was pitching to a client a huge software build project that was clearly going to take months of work, someone on their bid evaluation team asked in all seriousness if we couldn't just get it built in a weekend by using agile and buying the developers lots of pizza.

Whilst anyone can work speedily for a short time, it's very hard to maintain that sort of pace indefinitely. The speedier you become, the less sustainable it is. This is not to say that agile is not closely connected with the concept of speed. It absolutely is, just as it is connected with being more spontaneous in the work your produce and working more simply too. However, the important point is that while using agile can very much lead you to become more speedy, spontaneous and simple, these things are a consequence of agile, not the same as it.

Now, this may seem like a pedantic point, but it matters for two reasons. First, if agile focuses on outcomes, then to confuse the agile outcomes with the agile process is to do exactly the opposite. Agile is an approach that leads you to achieve the things you want to achieve, but to make sure this is happening, you must focus on the achievements themselves. It would be all too easy to setup an agile process and think that all your speed, spontaneity and simplicity problems had been fixed, when in the background people pay lip service to it and don't really understand it. Then you wonder six months later why being at work still feels like wading through treacle.

It is worth saying that the opposite is also true. Speed and spontaneity aren't the same as agile. The fundamental truth behind this one is that no-one deliberately turns up to work wanting things to move slowly, to get buried in paperwork, to wait weeks for decisions then find none of their marketing activity seems to have had much impact. So as a result, merely demanding that the organisation be more 'agile' just by cutting out red tape, simplifying delivery procedures and tweeting some hastily thought up brand-based jokes when the Superbowl's on TV is nearly always doomed to fail. In both cases, you're play-acting at agile. You need both to follow the agile approach, and at the same time focus on achieving the beneficial outcomes of agility. One without the other is not the best outcome, nor is it likely to be very sustainable either.

The best way I have to sum all of this up is to say that:

> *'Agility is no more the same as speed, spontaneity and simplicity than jogging is the same as being fit, healthy and thin. One can lead to the other, and often does, but it's by no means guaranteed.'* [20]

So if agile isn't the same as speed, then why do so many people say that it is, especially in the world of marketing and communications? We would be foolish to ignore such a common belief without at least examining where it might come from, in case there does happen to be some truth within it. Now, this is an area in need of further research, but I suspect there are at least three things going on here. The first is obviously confirmation bias. If people believe agility is the same as speed, they're going to see what they expect to see, and notice less the outcomes that don't conform with their expectations. Anything that happened more quickly is due to using agile, and anything that happened just as slowly, or even more slowly, is down to people not using agile properly. QED.

The second I suspect relates to the important issue of the specific microenvironment in which agile is being introduced. One thing that strikes me about the verbal case studies people give me about using agile, is how they generally all happen in a situation where something has gone wrong, or urgently needs fixing, or some other calamity has occurred. If you think about it, this is pretty logical, as if nothing were going wrong, why would anyone be thinking of swapping their standard approach for an agile approach? Agile has got itself a reputation for solving knotty problems quickly, so when a knotty problem happens, people try agile. The problem with this

[20] The author's shirt measurements and exercise regimen are available for inspection as proof of this point.

is that any problem that is both important and urgent generally gets people working more quickly anyway, cutting out distractions, red tape and lots of other delays in order to resolve the crisis. If agile only ever gets introduced in these situations, then it's bound to look like it's getting people working more quickly, even if it's just the situation itself that's causing this.

The third reason I suspect is closer to the reason why agile is more realistically seen as delivering positive outputs more quickly, in that as touched upon above, many of its components can't help but do so. If people collaborate rather than spend time negotiating contractual arrangements, then they cut out a lot of red tape and overhead. Likewise 'maximising the amount of work not done' is a pretty different focus to traditional approaches that is bound to cut out waste, inefficiency and delay. However, the problem here comes with whether this sort of approach is sustainable. If it is not, then even if things become super speedy in the short term, the approach is still not agile, and will ultimately fail in the medium to long term as people burn out, get fed up and leave the project.

So for me, agile is definitely something that can cause us to be quicker in what we do, but if we equate it just with being speedy, spontaneous and simple, we risk being mislead by our personal biases, ignoring the effects of our wider environment, or running an agile approach so hot that whilst it can celebrate short term wins, it ultimately causes a collapse in delivery. Perhaps a collapse so severe that in the longer term it cancels out any short-term gains in speed your project may have achieved.

If you conflate agile with speed, spontaneity and simplicity, you also risk destroying what chance you may have to implement it effectively from the outset. People are naturally skeptical about new ideas, especially new ideas presented to them by senior management or external consultants. So when you first move to an agile approach, they're going to be looking for as much validation as they can find that it's a bad idea. If you try to implement agile quickly, cut out parts of it you don't quite understand for the sake of simplicity and randomly chop and change how you use it for the sake of being spontaneous, then you're going to start making it look capricious, flexible to the point of meaninglessness, and probably quite stressful and annoying too. Besides, how many other organisation wide long-lasting cultural and mindset change programs have you heard of being implemented speedily, spontaneously and simply?

The elephant in the room for any agile consultant or advocate is also closely related to this point. Whilst the often quoted statistic that 70% of organisational change programs fail is quite probably apocryphal[21], few apocryphal stories are without any truth at all, and in the case of organisation change programs, I suspect the failure percentage is indeed quite high. Thus if we have to accept that change to an agile approach might well fail completely, then we must consider why it fails. Of course, there are numerous reasons for this, but for me, the one that really is a gigantic elephant is whether there are situations, environments, even cultures into which agile cannot be introduced at all. Personally, I don't believe enough research has been done on this question to give a conclusive answer, and there may very well never be one, but it is something we must consider. I've personally experienced agile projects that were just never going to work for a whole host of environmental, cultural or structural reasons. Not to say these barriers could not have been changed or removed, but like the philosopher's knife, you'd have to change so much of everything that you effectively end up just creating a whole new organisation, rather than changing an existing one.

---

[21] Hughes, M. (2011). 'Do 70 Per Cent of All Organizational Change Initiatives Really Fail?', *Journal of Change Management*, Vol. 11, No. 4, pp. 451–464 available to read online at http://www.tandfonline.com/doi/pdf/10.1080/14697017.2011.630506

So far, this has been a chapter largely looking at agile from the point of view either of software development, or as a theory in an of itself. So for a book about agile marketing and communications, this chapter is pretty light on the idea of agile within the context of marketing and communications themselves. Now worry not, there are a number of reasons for this. First, this whole book will be looking at agile in the context of marketing, so it seemed more important to get you understanding agile in and of itself first, before looking at how it might work in marketing. Coupled with this is the truth that not many people know how agile works in marketing yet. There will be pockets of excellence in it scattered across the world, but if the daily chatter about agile marketing online is anything to go by, there are just as many pockets of confusion and misunderstanding. Far better I think to understand agile in detail first, then look at how it could move across to marketing.

However, we cannot end this chapter without acknowledging some of the work and research that has been going on around agile marketing over the last few years. Now surprisingly there hasn't been too much published in this field to date, which is part of the motivation for this book. Unsurprisingly though, much of what has been published has been published online. I'm not here referring to the 'ebooks' that you can download in return for your email address, which turn out to be little more than a dozen PowerPoint slides with some brief ideas and a great deal of clipart. Rather, there's a seam of work that has happened over in the USA that resulted in something similar to the agile software development manifesto, but specifically called the agile marketing manifesto.

The agile marketing manifesto[22] is similar in form to the original agile software development manifesto, and looks like this.

[22] Taken from http://agilemarketingmanifesto.org

"We are discovering better ways of creating value for our customers and for our organizations through new approaches to marketing. Through this work, we have come to value:

- ***Validated learning*** *over* ***opinions and conventions***
- ***Customer focused collaboration*** *over* ***silos and hierarchy***
- ***Adaptive and iterative campaigns*** *over* ***Big-Bang campaigns***
- ***The process of customer discovery*** *over* ***static prediction***
- ***Flexible*** *vs.* ***rigid planning***
- ***Responding to change*** *over* ***following a plan***
- ***Many small experiments*** *over* ***a few large bets***"

Like the original, this manifesto also has a set of principles to support it, which read:

"Our highest priority is to satisfy the customer through early and continuous delivery of marketing that solves problems

We welcome and plan for change. We believe that our ability to quickly respond to change is a source of competitive advantage

Deliver marketing programs frequently, from a couple of weeks to a couple of months, with a preference to the shorter timescale

Great marketing requires close alignment with the business people, sales and development

Build marketing programs around motivated individuals. Give them the environment and support they need, and trust them to get the job done
Learning, through the build-measure-learn feedback loop, is the primary measure of progress

Sustainable marketing requires you to keep a constant pace and pipeline

Don't be afraid to fail; just don't fail the same way twice

Continuous attention to marketing fundamentals and good design enhances agility

Simplicity is essential"

The interesting thing in this manifesto is that it obviously has many similarities with the original, but also some distinct differences. On the first principle, whilst the original manifesto said 'valuable software' without defining what that value was, the marketing version of the manifesto suggests that the value of marketing lies in the degree to which it solves problems. On the second principle, the idea of speed has crept into the marketing manifesto, suggesting that they don't just welcome change, but respond to it quickly. Completely missing from the marketing manifesto is the original manifesto's recommendation that face-to face conversation is the most efficient and effective means of conveying information. Whilst both manifestos mention 'good design', they clearly mean different things in software development and marketing contexts. I also wonder if there is a degree of conservatism creeping into the marketing manifesto with its 'continuous attention to marketing fundamentals' too.

There is lots to consider in this proposed new manifesto, and potentially lots with which to disagree. Let us leave it there for now, and return to it later in the book, once we have considered how we might want to tackle marketing using agile if we were to approach it afresh.

Chapter 4 - The Big Idea

So then, now we've looked at what agile is, it seems important to spend some time looking at what it might be replacing in the world of marketing. Not only should this allow us to start to understand some of the challenges agile might face in replacing the current status quo, it should also allow us to understand whether these challenges are worth overcoming. After all, I am aware that agile marketing is a fashionable topic at the moment, one that is perhaps generating more excitement than substance. If we imagine that it is an idea moving through something like Roger's adoption curve (see diagram below[23]), then we are certainly no further forward than the 'early adopters' phase, and I suspect in many ways we are still in the 'innovators' phase right at the start.

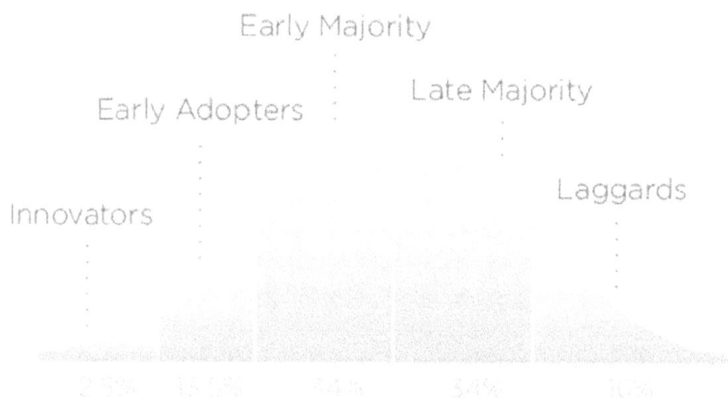

INNOVATION ADOPTION LIFECYCLE

As a result, we must exercise caution. Agile as a philosophy has yet to be extensively tested in the world of marketing and

---

[23] Diagram by Pnautilus on Wikipedia, CC BY 2.5, taken from http://upload.wikimedia.org/wikipedia/en/4/45/DiffusionOfInnovation.png

communications. Whilst innovators will need to create excitement in the concept to draw in the early adopters, it is likely that only by proving its value will the concept of agile marketing and communications move into the early majority stage. Whilst the signs are good, the value and applicability of agile and its methodologies to the world of marketing have yet to be proven. So too whole hearted a move towards it too early risks disturbing a current common industry approach that may have much to recommend it. But what then is the current approach of the marketing industry?

For the purposes of this book, I shall call the dominant industry approach 'the big idea'. This is a concept in need of further work and refinement, but I believe it encapsulates in just three words a lot of the current problems found in marketing and communications, especially as it explores the complex and uncertain environments of digital channels and media.

In my experience, marketers and comms people are all about the big idea. Here in the UK, Christmas comes early for marketers, as they wait excitedly to see what the big creative ideas will be for retail brands such as John Lewis and Marks & Spencer. I always find it interesting that people primarily get excited about the different creative ideas that come out in these campaigns, but rarely get as excited about the performance data the ideas generate over the following few months. If you look at many of the marketing and advertising industry awards that are given out, the write ups of the award winners typically focus on the idea, not the data around how the idea drove value to the business[24]. In short, without this clear focus on how marketing drives proven business value, and

---

[24] I particularly like this quote from the original 37 Signals Manifesto in this area - "37signals does not enter award competitions. - We believe that the marketing and communication awards "industry" encourages agencies to misplace their priorities on the opinions of their peers, rather than the needs of their clients' customers", taken from http://37signals.com/17.html

with its addiction to lauding big creative ideas before they've demonstrated any results, marketing currently is very un-agile. Now let me say at this early stage that I don't think that big ideas aren't worth having, or aren't effective. Clearly they can be. My father began his marketing career in the 1950's, when the expression 'Go to work on an egg' was rightly lauded as a superbly effective big idea for the UK's Egg Marketing Board. The fact that I, his son, still think of that line 60 years later, long after the demise of the Egg Marketing Board itself, is testament to this. Move on in time, and you get British Telecom's 'It's good to talk' campaign, that apparently delivered £5 billion in incremental sales for the company[25] and entered the every day language. Move to the present day, and, if you're reading this in the UK, what's the first animal you think of when you read the word 'simples'? The big idea behind the 'Compare the Meerkat' campaign was such a success that it unexpectedly turned a financial comparison site into one of the biggest toy manufacturers in the UK.

Big ideas clearly work, and to say we should get rid of them all together is a nonsense. However, I believe that the big idea has hidden within it a number of significant risks which can lead to the downfall of entire marketing campaigns and even organisations. The first is simple, in that the big idea has become so overly fetishized within the marketing industry that it has hidden the risks it contains. The second lies in the collection of practices and processes that this fetishization of the big idea has led to. These include the reliance on broad brush interruption marketing techniques, accepting wastage and inefficiency as inevitable, prioritising personal opinions and all their inherent biases over provable fact, then delivering all of this using a huge, linear and expensive approach to project management

---

[25] For an interesting account of the history of this campaign, visit http://www.campaignlive.co.uk/news/938629/

Let us start with the fetishization itself. This is an area on which I have yet to find much data collected, but in which I think it would be fascinating to see some further research undertaken. Big marketing or PR campaigns are currently primarily based around big ideas. If you ask someone to call to mind their favourite their favourite marketing campaigns of the last 10 years, chances are they will be able to sum them up in just a few words each. 'Compare the Meerkat', 'the Cadbury's Gorilla', 'Dancing Pony', 'Be More Dog'. This is fine, but if you think about it, this risks being hugely self re-enforcing. If the campaigns that people call to mind are those that can be summed up in one big idea, primarily because that's how marketing has been executed for a long time, then we all begin to think that we too need one big idea. The big idea then becomes the first and foremost goal of any marketing campaign, any brand story, and as long as you have one, people will think your organisation is headed in the right direction. Now, this is not wrong, but I believe it is not the whole story.

How people interact with brands, with organisations, with ideas, is far more complex than a simple test of memory recall on them will ever indicate. The product itself, the customer service, the price, upgrades, improvements, and many other factors will all influence which brands people choose to buy from and why. The other interesting thing you see here is the way big idea marketers talk about their consumers in terms of sweeping generalizations. Starting with the 'Baby Boomer' generation of the 1940's to the 1960's, we have since seen the rise of 'Generation X', 'Millennials' and now 'Generation Z' [26]. Marketers talk about these groups as if they really exist, as if they really do hold common, uniform sets of characteristics and behaviours, when of course the reality is far more complex. However, these sweeping generalisations are clearly appealing in their simplicity to a marketer who likes to

---

[26] See http://en.wikipedia.org/wiki/Generation#List_of_generations for more if you've an interest.

think in terms of simple big ideas. The creative matches the audience. Job done.

Now of course big idea based marketers would say this is an over simplification of their work. Many of them do take account of a whole range of factors external to the marketing campaign, and will indeed do research into these areas using surveys, focus groups, even economic theories in the process of shaping the idea. For example, a few big ideas may be thought up, and then run past a group of people believed to be statistically valid [27] to see which idea performs best amongst the target audience. However, individual focus group sessions need to be kept small if they are to be of use, thus collecting data from a large sample size can take a long time and be prohibitively expensive. In contrast, collecting data from a large sample of end users by putting multiple different ideas online can be done far more quickly and cheaply. As a result, digital campaigns suddenly allow numerous other factors to be considered and actively tested, far more than was the case in the traditional big idea days of marketing. In short, the big idea has always been a victim of its own environment, where campaigns were slow to deliver and data was expensive to collect. In contrast, the rise of digital and the Internet means any limitations we had around the feasibility of testing multiple ideas and seeing which work best have now largely been removed.

This leads us on to another interesting side effect of the big idea, measurability. Regardless of the cost and thus likelihood of end user research being carried out on traditional big idea campaigns, once the campaign has launched, it is really hard to measure how the big idea performs. I am always struck by the quotation attributed to Lord Leverhulme [28], which reads:

---

[27] If you're interested in the statistical validity of market research, or rather the very common failings with it, read Dataclysm by Christian Rudder.

[28] Or John Wanamaker, or Henry Ford, or many others. It appears unclear who the original utterer was, or indeed if they even existed at all.

"Half the money I spend on advertising is wasted; the trouble is I don't know which half"

Now whether this percentage is accurate, the broad principle seems undeniably to have been true in the earlier days of marketing. You put advertisements on TV or the radio, printed them in the press, put them on billboards, and watched to see if your sales increased. Whilst you could to some degree run consumer research to try to understand which of these channels was delivering the most return on investment for you, this was still a very broad-brush approach. People outside of your target audience would see your marketing, and you would have no idea how many people saw it, who these people were or when they saw it. As noted in Chapter 2, over time the channels became predictable and understood, but the understanding of them was effectively still quite broad brush. You knew what you had to do to achieve results, you just didn't understand the impact of each press ad, each TV slot or each billboard down to the finest level of detail. How could you? Besides, as long as things were working, why waste time and profits on the expense of massively detailed research?

Digital marketing has changed all of this dramatically, and only looks to change it even further as technology advances. Thanks to the fact that numerous different sites, especially Facebook, have caused so many people to post information about their demographics, interests and buying behaviours on the Internet, you can now take huge strides to reduce wastage in your marketing campaigns, showing them only to people in your target audience, or only to a subset of that audience that you know to be currently in market for your product, even only to someone in your target audience who is currently in market when they happen to be within six feet of your high street store. Some have been arguing that the 'Half the money I spend on advertising is wasted' aphorism has been dying for some time, and regardless of when it started dying, I think it is clear that if technology continues to advance in the way it has, it will eventually wither away altogether. Even if you still do advertising that does not lead to sales, and you almost certainly will [29], at least you will know which advertising it has been.

In the 'olden days' of marketing, it wasn't just measurability of the channel that was an issue, it was also the ability to tailor the messages you put out through your channels.

Clearly, when marketers only had certain well-established channels through which to deliver their message, a message based on one big idea was a good fit. Say you wanted to create a TV ad. You would know that that would only be shown on the small handful of commercial TV channels that existed, and would be shown to everyone watching that channel regardless of their age, gender, location, social status or any other factor. Essentially, so many of the variables that might have affected how your marketing was interpreted in the head of the recipient were out of your control. All you could do was create one single message that you hoped would land with impact in the head of the broad target audience you had identified, then put it out there for indiscriminate consumption. The same was largely true for print advertising too. Admittedly there may have been more newspapers in existence than TV channels back in the day, themselves targeting different demographics, thus allowing in theory the production of different messages for different audiences. However, it was still a very broad-brush approach, with little ability to refine messaging to suit individual types of consumer on a more one to one basis. In essence, you still needed a big idea, one that would catch the attention and stick in the mind, in what Seth Godin describes as the era of interruption marketing [30].

---

[29] If we ever reach a point where every piece of advertising leads to a purchase by anyone who sees it, we will likely be living in the days foretold by the film 'Minority Report' - http://en.wikipedia.org/wiki/Minority_Report_(film)

[30] Godin, S. (1999). *Permission marketing*, Sydney: Simon and Schuster.

Now, the new digital age allows marketers to target multiple different messages at much more tightly defined groups of individuals, defined by numerous demographic, interest-based, environmental and behavioural criteria. As a result, you don't just need one big idea to tell people. Indeed, if you took this approach you'd miss so many of the opportunities and benefits that digital and the Internet give you. With such fine-grained targeting now at your fingertips, you can target difference messages at different consumers, messages that will work best in different small categories of consumers. For example, even if your target audience already feels quite well defined, say 16-25 year olds living in cities, they might still respond differently to messages at 9am than they might at 2am. Previously, your printed messages existed in the same form all day. Now, your digital messages can change in tone, style any numerous other factors as the day goes on[31].

Of course, all of these different messages might look odd and reduce message recall if they weren't all based around the same core proposition. A firm that one minute is selling its dog food on the strength of its premium quality is going to muddy its message if it switches to competing on price the next. An underlying brand image or product narrative is still needed to give direction and clarity to the messaging produced, no matter how tailored and extensively nuanced those messages may be. However, the fact that messages can now be so much better targeted, and their impact so

---

[31] One interesting example of this sort of thing happening in the pre-digital days if found in political marketing. Politicians and political parties are notorious for tailoring their messages to suit their audience, promising different things to different people, often down to quite a fine grained level of detail. However, they could only manage it due to the peculiar way politics is often conducted face to face, allowing demographic data to be gathered and messages specifically tailored in real time. I've yet to meet any professional marketer who goes around door to door selling their message every day, every evening and every weekend in the way successful politicians do. I'd love to hear of any other similar examples that you may know about.

much better understood, means the days of the 'one size fits all' big idea, created up front, published everywhere, with an acceptance that it contained huge amounts of wastage, are now very much numbered.

For all the benefits that digital marketing now affords, there is a theme emerging here that points clearly at its downsides too. For if the old big idea days of marketing had one thing going for them, it was clearly that they were simple and stable. You knew how many channels you had and the sort of campaigns that worked on them, even if you didn't have detail down to the micro level. However, whilst the data you had access to was limited, it was all the more simple as a result, and so easier to work with and easier to understand. There wasn't much change in the number or types of channels either, so you got to build learnings over time. Just as the fact that gravity doesn't change allows an architect to build predictably successful big ideas in brick and stone, the fact that the marketing landscape was far more stable and less complex made having simple big ideas far more effective. In contrast, as we have seen already, the digital marketing environment is far more recent, more complex, less well understood and, possibly permanently, more difficult to understand. Surely this change alone gives us a reason to ask whether the big idea approach to marketing is still valid?

Now the reason I ask this question is because I don't believe it is as rhetorical as it sounds. If digital and the Internet are changing the marketing landscape and practice as profoundly as I have set out above, then this potentially challenges many marketers, especially those later in their careers at senior levels, who have spent their lives believing in upfront planning and the big idea approach. This is worth discussing, as it relates to the often unmentioned issue in any way of working, the issue of power and bias. We touched upon this issue in the previous chapter when we looked at how agile practice is passed from person to person more than it is written and

codified, but all of us contain internal biases as to how we see the world and interpret information we are given. Some of them we are aware of, some of them we can discover, some we may never notice we have at all. These biases mean that any marketing decisions are going to be coloured and shaped by our interpretation of the information available. I believe this is the issue that might be most unsettling about the rise of digital marketing, and the most threatening to those used to traditional big idea approaches.
First, data trumps and exposes bias. If, in the traditional big ideas days, not much data was available, then bias was a lot less visible. You'd never be able to tell if the billboard poster that your director loved worked better than the other one the creative team preferred. Not only because the director's preferred poster would be the only one that got released in public, given the 'one size fits all' approach to channels, but even if both did go out, there wasn't a lot of data available to understand which performed better than the other anyway. Nowadays, rather than the marketing decisions being taken on the basis of personal power, hierarchy and opinion, and thus being affected by personal bias, each option in the decision can be quickly tested online. Accurate performance data can then be collected and the superior one released more widely as part of the main campaign. I suspect this tension between power, hierarchy, personal opinion and instant large-scale data will be a significant blocker to the spread of agile in the field of marketing and communications. That said, I would suggest that even if this issue doesn't arise due to the implementation of agile itself, the mere presence of improved data will in and of itself increasingly bring the tensions to a head over time.

The other risk with agile in relation to power is how it might start to change who holds power and how they do so in the traditional big idea world. Big ideas that prove to be a runaway success are currently so loved and sought after that people want to be seen to be the one to come up with it; to make their career by devising a killer campaign. Equally, no one wants to be the person that turned down a successful big idea. Having the right opinion brings profile, power and profit, things many people seem to think are important goals for their short time on this planet. The thing is though, how often are these right opinions genuinely genius pieces of thinking, and how often are they just luck? As Marwood points out in the film Withnail and I;

> "*Even a stopped clock tells the right time twice a day.*"

Besides, who's defining success anyway? If you can't see in much detail which marketing assets worked better than others, then the only thing you can celebrate is the big idea itself, further reinforcing the bias towards that approach. If we stopped celebrating big ideas and started instead using far more data in our assessment of success, then we would devalue a huge amount of the prestige awarded to the lucky winners under the old system.

So then, we have examined in some detail how the current big idea approach to marketing has come to be and how it has existed for so long. But if you think about it, what we have been talking about so far has been in the area of marketing ideas and creativity. What about the day job? Actually delivering a marketing campaign takes an awful lot of planning, project management, budget management and all sorts of other routine day-to-day practices. I think this is likely one of the other significant sticking points for the implementation of an agile marketing approach into a big idea world. If the death of the big idea challenges those at the top, the death of delivering campaigns in a big idea manner is equally challenging to those at lower levels.

You see, I don't think the advertising industry is alone taking a big idea approach to life. In many ways, it has been just as subject to the same trends that have been affecting all industries since the end of the Second World War. Modern western project management has its roots in the project management methodologies developed to deliver large military, construction and space flight projects by government and the military following the Second World War [32]. For these projects, predictability, safety and cost management were vital given the size and profile of the work being undertaken. Understandably, this was a project management approach that fitted the world of marketing quite effectively too. When there were few channels, and much about them was predictable, proven and understood, at least at a broad level, then a project management technique designed for predictability, safety and cost management was quite appealing.

However, in the new digital age, are the same project management techniques that put men on the moon applicable to the kinds of low budget, low risk, uncertain and exploratory work that the complex digital environment both allows and requires? How can project management techniques designed to prevent failures in space shuttles promote the 'fail fast' or 'move fast and break things' culture that many digital marketers are currently seeking? It is instructive is it not, that the well-known project management methodology called PRINCE2 stands for 'PRojects In Controlled Environments'. How can this approach be meaningfully applied to the digital age if, as we have seen, digital environments are anything but controllable or predictable?

It is here that we can see one of the first warning signs that digital was changing the established order, but it is a sign that non-digital marketers probably missed at the time. When software development first started, especially once it started to grow in scale and budget, it needed a methodology for managing the development process. Presumably seeing no issue with the status quo, and having no other methodology to apply, early software developers used a methodology called Waterfall, which is in many

[32] Chin, G. (2004). *Agile project management: how to succeed in the face of changing project requirements*. New York: AMACOM.

ways similar to PRINCE2 in its love of upfront planning, extensive documentation, application of process and careful monitoring of timescales[33]. Now if you look at any number of the big IT projects undertaken in the UK, especially in Government, there have been some catastrophic failures using Waterfall approaches. In a fascinating report that I recommend you read, McKinsey found that:

"On average, large IT projects run 45 percent over budget and 7 percent over time, while delivering 56 percent less value than predicted."

It went on to add that:

"17 percent of IT projects go so bad that they can threaten the very existence of the company." [34]

For me, events like these were the early warning signal that things might not be quite right in our predominant ways of thinking and working when we apply them to the digital world. I believe this warning signal is now going off in the world of marketing and communications too, as the digital world expands into it. Indeed, the line between software developer and marketer has blurred hugely over the last 10 years. On the Internet, a great user interface for your website, keeping the site really simple and making sure it meets all the most important needs of the vast majority of users are all as much marketing activities as they are software development ones. In contrast, for all the occasional viral successes [35], I'm sure

---

[33] The wikipedia article on Waterfall is actually quite good if you want to find out more - http://en.wikipedia.org/wiki/Waterfall_model

[34] Taken from Bloch, M., Blumberg, S. & Laartz, J. (2012) 'Delivering large-scale IT projects on time, on budget, and on value', available at http://www.mckinsey.com/insights/business_technology/delivering_large-scale_it_projects_on_time_on_budget_and_on_value

[35] It's also interesting, is it not, that very often viral Internet campaigns are produced by individuals or small groups not using a formal project management

we can all think of numerous big idea, big budget marketing campaigns that have singularly failed to cross over into the digital world. So I think it follows that we would do well to look at the project management approach that software developers have used to adapt to the digital world, as that digital world increasingly expands into the world of marketing.

But if we're looking here at the impacts of agile on those on the delivery side of the marketing campaign, what might those impacts be? Now of course, overall there will be numerous impacts that manifest in numerous different ways. From changes in the number and format of their regular meetings to greater trust amongst co-workers and even bigger cultural phenomena that alter their entire realities in significant ways. I think though, alongside the loss of a Waterfall mentality, one of the changes will be most immediately noticed are around what is known as the iron triangle. Versions of it vary, but in essence it looks like this:

methodology, whilst very rarely are they produced by large organisations using formal project management.

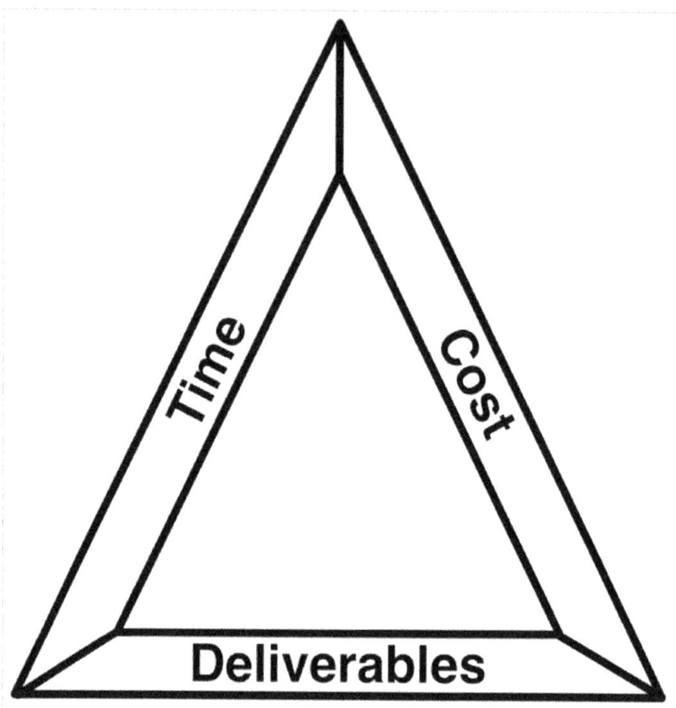

I suspect looking at that, you're thinking all three sides of the triangle are equally important. Conventional wisdom is that you have to deliver every deliverable you said your marketing campaign would deliver, and do it on time and on budget. The equilateral triangle makes sense. Time, cost and deliverables are all equally important, so each side of the triangle is the same size. The thing is, as much as we kid ourselves that this is what we're doing, I believe that in fact we naturally prioritise. Whilst it would be lovely if we could always deliver everything we say we will on time and on budget, in reality some of these factors take priority over others. But which?

Whether you're client side or agency side, think about the last campaign you ran. If you're client side, I suspect time was a hugely important consideration for you. You've been tasked with launching the company's Christmas campaign, so it can't go live in January. Likewise, if you're agency side, there's no fun in phoning up a client a telling them their campaign has been delayed. People shout at you, you look bad, so time is obviously hugely important.

Then think of cost. If you're client side, you don't want to be seen to go back to your boss to ask for more money, or explain why you've overspent your budget. Likewise if you're agency side, asking clients for an increase in budget for the same amount of deliverables you originally promised is a difficult conversation. If your client doesn't agree to it, then you'll have to take the hit and let the campaign eat into your profit margins, losing you kudos with your agency bosses. So, on either side, cost obviously can't change either.

Now this is fine when the environment is stable and predictable. In this environment, marketing activity is likely to be largely a repeat of some previous activity the marketing team has already carried out. Different creative of course, but having used the same channels over the years, you know pretty well how long delivery takes and how much it costs. You also know what you can deliver for that time and cost, so your deliverables generally get delivered in full. Now, this obviously doesn't always happen 100% of the time, but you can clearly see that predictable delivery of planned deliverables on time and on budget is more likely in stable, predictable and well-understood marketing channels.

However, in a complex, rapidly changing and largely unknown environment, the iron triangle becomes so much harder to manage. Costs become less knowable, as do timescales. But if we've said that time and cost are the two most important sides of the triangle which cannot be changed, then all you can flex and fail to deliver on is deliverables. I suspect this is why many digital campaigns fail to get off the ground when delivered using a traditional Waterfall mindset. If the complex and uncertain nature of the digital environment means that you can't be certain about the time and the cost, and you eventually find you've estimated them wrong, then the easiest thing to do is often to change the deliverables and just abandon the work, hoping that nobody notices or particularly minds.

Sadly, if the activity is digital, then the chances are they may not do so, as the senior people who are paid to mind never really understood what the activity was all about anyway. They watch TV and read newspapers, so will notice if the press and TV ads don't get delivered, but if the Facebook campaign ends up falling by the wayside, then they'll only notice if their kids happen to mention it. Besides, if you're micro-targeting numerous different messages in different digital channels, then it's much harder to make sure each one gets delivered anyway. If a Facebook ad is targeted only at people located in Manchester, how will the London based marketing department ever know whether it went live or not?

However, let's pause a minute here to think about deliverables, as it's actually a word with multiple meanings. On the one hand it can mean physical marketing assets. You say your campaign will deliver a TV ad, some press ads, some digital display and a radio partnership. Those are all deliverables. On top of this though, surely another set of deliverables is the results that your campaign delivers, be they sales, brand reputation, visits to your website or any number of different performance indicators? The difference between these two types of deliverables is one of timescale.

If you deliver your TV, press, digital or any other assets late, that will be noticed immediately. You've booked the TV slots, but have no ad to play out in them. Massive fail. However, if your TV ads don't deliver the sales you expected them to, that probably won't be noticed until a few months later. Plenty of time then to explain away why things haven't gone as expected. Perhaps the campaign environment changed. Perhaps a competitor came out with a similar ad at the same time, muddying your message. Perhaps your entire market went through an unexpected dip, which has led to fewer sales than you expected. Besides, in traditional channels you'll never know in any great detail which specific ad or channel it was that failed more than others. Whatever the scenario, your campaign not delivering much business value is easier to explain away than missing actual delivery dates, running over budget or just straight up not delivering an asset or assets that you said you would.

However, is this really good enough as an approach? Surely the only point of marketing is to drive sales, product recall, brand consideration and all the rest? If your marketing isn't doing these things, why are you even doing it? I'd thus like to suggest that the iron triangle should actually look something like this.

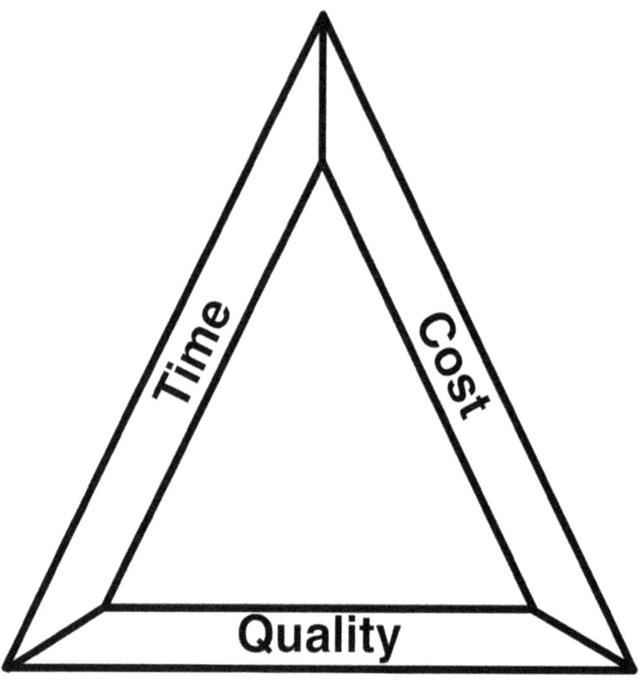

Do you see what's happened? We've replaced 'Deliverables' with 'Quality'. They're closely related of course, and are both closely related to issues of time and cost, but there's a significant difference. In a big idea world, with more focus on creative execution than on creative performance, deliverables are what matter. You've planned and created assets for what everyone believes to be a great campaign based around a killer big idea, so all that's left to do is create the deliverables. In an agile world, more focused on actual results and demonstrable business value, creating the deliverables is far less important than creating quality deliverables.

Now, it would be lovely if all three of these; time, cost and quality; could be delivered perfectly, but as mentioned before, doing so in a complex and uncertain digital environment is far more difficult. So something's got to give somewhere. However, we've already seen that you can't be seen to deliver your campaign late, and you can't run over budget or eat into your budget or profit margin, so what's left to flex? Well, it's quality. If you can't change time or budget, quality is the one side of the triangle that has to flex when operating in a complex and unknown environment in order to accommodate the immovability of the other two.

However, if agile states that quality should be our most important goal [36], then those delivering the campaign will have to get their heads around the idea that, in an complex and unknown digital environment, time and cost might have to become the factors they flex. This is hugely difficult with a standard project management mindset, as if you tell senior people used to predictability that you want to run a marketing campaign, but are not that interested in how much it will end up costing or when it will get delivered, well, that's a hard discussion to have. What I suggest then, is that the best response to this is to find a new approach that reassures people at all levels by regularly delivering small amounts of value, constantly optimising and maximising the value as it goes. Time and cost are expensive, but they often become far more flexible if you can prove that you're flexing them to deliver greater value more regularly than the old approach.

This of course causes another change in the way people delivering marketing campaigns start to view them. Previously, if time was a hugely important factor, then it was so because it contained fixed delivery dates. If you need to start flexing time, then you need to start flexing and moving your delivery dates. But a delivery date

[36] It is worth noting the presence of the word 'valuable' in principle one of the agile manifesto, which states "Our highest priority is to satisfy the customer through early and continuous delivery of *valuable* software" whilst principle nine states "Continuous attention to technical excellence and good design enhances agility". Both of these principles thus point to the fact that quality is, or at least should be, an over riding concern of an agile practitioner.

that moves too many times is just a date. So if the delivery date effectively no longer exists, then the campaign never technically launches. This is of course one of the logical conclusions of an agile response to complex and uncertain digital marketing environments. Rather than planning, designing and creating all your marketing assets before launch, you just regularly produce assets, see how they perform, then use the data you've collected to inform the creation of some more. This is especially true if we want to target much better defined subsets of our audience with multiple different types of creative, each tailored to its audience subset. Is it any surprise that the last few years have seen the rise of the phrase 'always on' or 'always there' marketing? Marketers have clearly identified this phenomenon, but I believe they can only make best use of it when they tailor their creative and delivery approaches to fit the new reality. To my mind, agile feels like an excellent approach for enabling this.

So it looks as though, in a constantly evolving digital world, a big idea approach to marketing is a pretty risky bet. But there is one big problem with this. Big ideas clearly still happen, and they clearly still work, at least sometimes. Despite the many issues with them in the new digital world, we would be foolish to ignore their worth or throw them away entirely. In fact, I don't actually see a complete clash between the big idea and agile. For me, agile is still about aiming at a big idea, but doing it from the bottom up, not the top down. Less planning and up front decision making, less personal opinion, with power and responsibility devolved from senior to more junior levels, and everyone being open to changes in direction as new information emerges. By pivoting quickly to follow successes, eventually your work will start to take shape and look like a big idea, but one with more fluidity and responsiveness, and one with a greater focus on delivering real business value above all else, as proven by hard data not industry awards.

I personally think this all sounds pretty appealing. So next, let's look at how you turn agile from a philosophy into a process for creating and delivering responsive, successful marketing campaigns.

Chapter 5 - The Scrum Process

As we have seen then, agile itself isn't a methodology. It's far more of a philosophy, a mindset, an approach to working collaboratively with others to chart new terrain in an uncertain environment. Whilst understanding and embracing this is hugely important to adopting an agile approach to your marketing, it doesn't really tell you what you need to do day to day to live this dream.

In order to turn agile from a philosophy into a practice, a number of different methodologies have been developed. I say 'have been' developed, but if you think back to the history of the agile manifesto we covered above, a number of these methodologies were already being practiced before the manifesto was written. Indeed, it was in many ways this manifesto that brought together the different methodologies into a coherent philosophy.

As such, in the software world, there are a number of different methodologies that can be used to implement agile. These include eXtreme Programming (XP), Crystal, Scrum, Adaptive Software Development, Dynamic Systems Development Method, Feature-Driven Development, lean development and agile RUP. Now, it should immediately be stated that some of these methodologies are, at least currently, specifically for software. They are to a greater or lesser extent unlikely to have been tested as methodologies for delivering marketing campaigns. This is not to say each of them could not be repurposed into the world of marketing, rather that they are, as yet, not very well tested for marketing delivery.

Two things follow on from this fact. First, in any attempt to implement an agile methodology, consideration must be given as to whether the methodology is correct for the tasks at hand. It is all too easy to follow the latest fashions, and see an agile methodology as the pot of gold at the end of the rainbow, a pot temptingly buried in the greener grass of the other side. However, as we considered above, the existing environment and organisational culture matter, so if you want to implement one of the agile methodologies, careful consideration needs to be given as to which one you implement, in what environment and how.

This is not to say that there are no commonalities between the different agile methodologies. At their heart, all of them focus on small teams, collaboration, flexibility, iterative delivery, constant output, constant testing, feedback and gradually approaching the end goal in incremental steps. To be honest, I suspect a lot of the argument about which methodology is superior is a lot like the People's Front of Judea hating on the Judean People's Front in Monty Python's 'The Life Of Brian'; a victim of Sayre's Law, which states;

"*In any dispute, the intensity of feeling is inversely proportional to the value of the issues at stake.*" [37]

In other words, the less things matter, the more people argue.

Still, I wouldn't say you could just pick up any old agile software development methodology and apply it to a marketing or communications campaign you're running without any thought. The methods share many commonalities, but are also each different in some important regards. Fundamentally they're written for software development too, so if you started looking to implement Feature Driven Development to develop a TV ad, you'd soon be wondering where your configuration management system comes into the picture.

So, which methodology should you choose to get started with agile? Well, I'd recommend the one called scrum, for a number of reasons. First, scrum is very well known and widely used amongst

[37] http://en.wikipedia.org/wiki/Sayre's_law

the software development community, and as a result is well tested in a number of different contexts and environments. Second, it gives you a nice way to structure your team and the meetings they have[38]. As we see throughout this book, implementing a new organisational philosophy and methodology is tricky, so following scrum gives people a clear signal from the start that the fundamentals of the way they work have changed. If you stop sitting down in meetings, have a visual board anyone can look at to see the progress of your work, and have a time boxed opportunity for people to review your campaign assets, then those in and around the team see clearly from the start that change is happening.

My final reason for choosing scrum is more subjective. I like scrum. I've used it a lot, and seen great results come out of it. I also believe that out of all the available methodologies, scrum is the one that most easily crosses over into the world of marketing, especially digital and content marketing. However, I'd be fascinated to hear from anyone who's taken other agile methodologies across into their marketing activities, and I intend to do further research into this myself over the coming years. For example, the pair programming approach found in the eXtreme Programming methodology might have interesting parallels with the 'war room' approach some organisations are starting to use to produce marketing content in real-time. However, for the purposes of this book, I'll be advocating that you adopt a scrum methodology as your first step into turning agile from a philosophy into a practice.

---

[38] The term scrum is actually borrowed from the game of rugby. It's not an analogy I shall spend time exploring here, but it can help to have an image in your mind of what a rugby scrum looks like when you're imagining how a scrum team operates. Just try not to focus on the kicking, punching and shouting that goes on in a rugby scrum. It's not a key component of an agile scrum, although it has sadly been known to happen when some people think other people are 'Getting. Scrum. Wrong.'.

So what is scrum? Well, before getting into it I should caution you that the explanation of it given in this book will necessarily be brief, incomplete and tailored more specifically for a marketing and communications audience, based on my experience of applying it directly to marketing, PR and communications. If you want to get into scrum in more detail, and look at some of how it relates more specifically to software development too, then I'd absolutely recommend books like '*Essential Scrum: A Practical Guide to the Most Popular Agile Process*' by Ken Rubin and '*Agile Product Management with Scrum: Creating Products That Customers Love*' by Roman Pichler. Both are fantastic books, which I hope I can inspire you to read through my discussion of scrum in this book.

So, in short, scrum is a project management technique that uses an agile mindset to deliver continuous outputs through repeated short cycles of activity called sprints. In each sprint, the team working on the marketing campaign runs through a series of regular meetings, during which they decide what they will work on, work on it collaboratively together, discovering, planning and designing as they go, all whilst keeping an eye on what to work on next. They are also regularly reviewing what they've produced and reviewing the process they used to produce it, with a view to improving it in the next sprint. A top line flowchart is given below to illustrate what I believe to be the stages of the scrum methodology when applied to a marketing campaign.

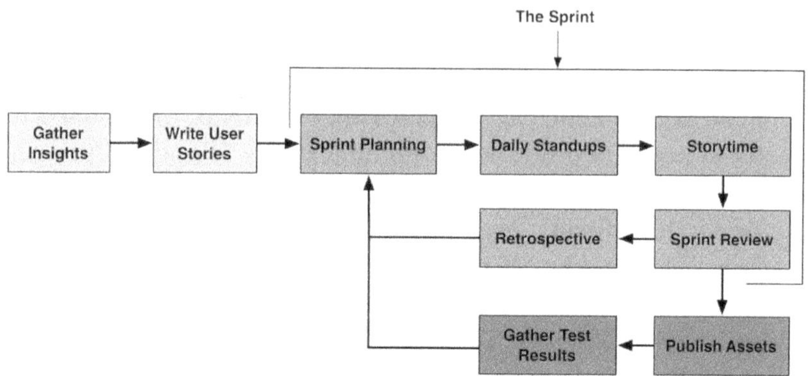

Whilst the scrum team is ideally quite small, seven plus or minus two people being the recommended rule of thumb, it also has a number of specific roles for people within those teams. These roles are product owner, scrum master and team member, although as ever with things agile, some implementations of scrum sometimes vary these roles and add some additional ones in to suit their specific purposes. For now though, in the spirit of keeping things simple that agile advocates, let's just look at scrum methodology with these three main types of role.

Before we get to them though, I was to mention something scrum has in it that I love, and something I think that helps scrum transfer across into the world of marketing quite easily [39]. It's called a user story, and after all, what marketer doesn't like telling and working with stories?

The User Story

In my opinion, the user story is central to the whole process of scrum in the context of marketing and communications. Here, I

[39] Although as an interesting example of the flexibility of agile methodologies, user stories didn't actually originate in scrum, but actually originated in eXtreme programming.

must confess a bias. I adore user stories. No matter whether I'm working on software development, writing content marketing or writing a book, user stories are perfect little nuggets of information that help take my work to the next level. Why then do they get me so excited?

In essence, a user story is a way of capturing a user requirement for whatever it is you're working on. So in the world of software, if you were designing some sort of membership based website, you'd need a user story that captured the requirement of people to log in to your site. In the world of marketing, if you were producing some content for a social media channel, you'd need various user stories to explain the sorts of people your content will be aimed at, the types of information they need and what they want to do with that information.

The thing each of these stories has in common however is that they're based on real user needs. If big idea marketing is as full of personal opinion and bias as I believe it to be, then user stories are the complete opposite. When you create marketing assets using user stories, you put your target audience front and centre of your considerations, not your creative director's personal opinion, or your managing director's desire to produce something that will impress the judges at whatever award ceremony is currently in fashion.

This very much ties in with how agile has the delivery of quality and value at its heart. If you remember back to earlier in this book, the first principle of the agile manifesto states that:

"Our highest priority is to satisfy the customer through early and continuous delivery of valuable software."

Notice this is about satisfying the customer, not the creative director, your marketing peers or a panel of judges for an industry award. User stories give you an excellent focus on seeing the customer as your first and foremost priority. Theirs is the opinion that now counts more than any other.

User stories are really simple too, and are typically composed of three elements:

"As a...
I want to...
So that..."

So for example, if you were writing a user story for a generic marketing asset to promote a product that saves people time, a user story might look like this:

"As a father with a busy diary,
I want to find out how this product saves me time,
So that I can spend more time with my children."

Now, that's a somewhat simplified example. Indeed user stories are often hard to get utterly perfect, but it's good enough for now. So let's consider each of the three components of a user story in turn, in order to unpick how they work in more detail.

"As a..."

This is the first line of a user story, the one that sets out who the story aims to satisfy, often called the persona. This persona is typically an end user of whatever you're producing, hence the name 'user story', and by placing it at the start of your story, you're really making the point that your work is all about your end users. In marketing, I suspect this first part of a user story is generally quite easy to write. After all, you've done your market research on who your target audience is, or you've run the numbers to understand which people are currently buying your products. So you should pretty easily be able to set out the personas your user stories are for. Right?

"I want to..."

This second part of a user story sets out what it is the user identified in the first part wants to do. So, it may be finding out which products you offer, or finding out how to save time in their day with your product, or just how to buy your products. In essence, if you can think of something someone would like to do with the thing you're producing, then you can write it into a user story.

"So that..."

Having said that the first and second parts of a user story are often pretty easy to write, this third part of the user story is sometimes the most tricky of the three. In it, you need to set out why the type of user you've identified would want to be able to do the thing you think they want to do. To take some marketing examples, perhaps people want to find out where they can buy your product at the cheapest price so they can save money on their next purchase. Or perhaps they want to find out what after sales service you offer, so they can feel reassured that they're covered if anything goes wrong. Perhaps they just want to see how your different products compare with each other, so they can choose the one that's right for them.

For me, it's this third part of the user story that's the most useful, as it's the one that most steers you away from big idea marketing, and towards an agile process of constant exploration, testing, collaborating and learning, letting your plan emerge as you go. For it is only when you understand *why* someone wants to do what they want to do that you can come up with a solution that best meets their needs. Often, it may be that the solution you first think of isn't necessarily the only one, or indeed the best one, for meeting that user's need.

Take for example a domestic scenario. A wife comes home to find that her entirely unreconstructed husband hasn't done the washing up. The conversation runs as follows:

Wife: "Darling, could you do the washing up please?"
Husband: "Not now, I'm busy"
W: "What? But the washing up always needs doing! Just get it done!"
H: "Oh FFS, I really haven't got time right now, do it yourself"
Divers alarums, exeunt omnes...

Now, if the wife had presented her request as a user story, this conversation might have run a little differently:

Wife: "Darling, as a house-proud lady who is having some friends round this evening, I want to see that there aren't dishes strewn around the kitchen, so that I can avoid feeling embarrassed when my friends come round in an hour"

Husband: "Ah ok, I didn't realise that you wanted the dishes doing so urgently because your friends were coming round, let's look to fix this problem. It seems like there are a few different solutions we could consider though. One is washing the dishes, but you actually just want the kitchen to look tidy when your friends come round. So if I wash everything up now, there will still be dishes everywhere being left out to dry. How about I just gather up all the dirty dishes, stick them in a bin bag and stash that under the sink so your friends won't see them when they come round? Alternatively, I could just chuck the dishes in the big bin outside and buy some new ones when I go into town tomorrow."

Now, I accept the husband in this situation is coming up with some absurd solutions, and the idea of a married couple communicating in user stories is equally absurd. However, it illustrates the point that working in user stories really allows you to focus in on user needs, the 'why' or 'what's in it for me' question that's too often left out of big idea marketing. It also allows you to come up with a number of different options for meeting your users' needs, and consider each in turn to find the likely best solution. In doing this, the user story promotes real creativity, as every possible solution should be considered to solve the problem, rather than starting with a specification that fixes preconceptions about what should and should not be done. Even better, in helping you come up with these different options, it allows you to create some variations of each marketing asset to test out with real end users, rather than just going with the 'best' idea you came up with. Because user stories now force the customer to be front and centre of your considerations when producing marketing assets, they not only help you produce more ideas, they also remove your risk of reverting to your comfort zone in the complex and uncertain marketing environments in which we now operate.

The other fascinating thing that happens with user stories is the degree to which they provide a check and balance on your internal biases. I've occasionally run exercises where I've tried to retrofit user stories onto existing marketing campaigns with assets that have already been planned and designed, and the results are always fascinating. Every time, the process of creating user stories for existing campaigns has resulted in two things.

First, you find that not every aspect of the campaign can have a user story written for it. You might be able to write the 'As a..' and 'I want to...' elements of the story, but you get completely stuck when writing the 'So that...' part. A user story is not a user story if you cannot write all three elements of it, so any activity you do, or asset you produce, that can't fill in each of the three elements is very likely something you should no longer bother doing. Why

produce marketing that isn't aimed at a specific audience, or doesn't contain any value proposition for them?
The other thing that happens when retrofitting user stories to existing work is that you generally come up with some new user stories you didn't think of when planning the original campaign and its assets. The rigour of understanding every facet of your audience, understanding what they want to do and why they want to do it, often flags up some types of user or user needs that you've thus far entirely neglected, sparking new ideas for stories. Try it yourself sometime, I promise you'll find improvements in what you're currently doing.

Hopefully by now you've understood what user stories are and why they're so useful. However, whilst they can sound simple in principle, one tricky element of user stories is getting the level of detail right. Take these two examples:

"*As a person looking to save time in my busy day,*
I want to read some advice on saving time,
So that I can have more time doing the things I enjoy"

"*As a 47 year old man called Bob who lives in Saffron Walden,*
I want to be able to spend less time keeping my socks in matching pairs after I wash them,
So that I can make sure I only wear black socks when at work, but wear more colourful socks at the weekend, making happier use of the time I have saved on pairing socks"

Now, these are both user stories, and both on the same topic of saving time, but they massively differ in the level of detail they provide, and so the potential scale of your solution. The first story could see you producing marketing content on a huge range of different timesaving topics for the next ten years or more. The second could lead you to produce content that is so specific to Bob's individual needs that it is largely irrelevant to anyone else, and you may as well just phone him to let him know the solution. It might also lead to you wasting time yourself, researching how the sock-pairing needs of 47 year old men in Saffron Walden differ from the sock-pairing needs of 22 year old women living in Sixpenny Handley.

Typically, when people first start writing user stories, they start out pretty large like that first example. Stories this large are known, appropriately enough, as 'epic stories'. They're useful for setting the direction of travel for a marketing campaign, giving you enough of a thing to aim at without tying you down to a specific 'big idea' or creative execution right from the start. However, if you tried to deliver all of the assets to meet the story in just two weeks, you'd rapidly come up against so many obstacles that the work would just fall apart.

As a result, you need to break these epic stories down into multiple smaller stories, ones that are capable of being worked on in a meaningful way. That said though, you can go too far in the opposite direction. The more you start to break down user stories into smaller chunks, the more you run the risk of ending up back in the 'big idea' space, planning all of your campaign deliverables up front in minute detail and leaving you no room for discovering the best deliverable through the process of delivering the work itself.

Alternatively, what can happen as you start to introduce scrum to a traditional 'big idea' marketing organisation is that people are so used to seeing big ideas that they refuse to see each individual story as anything other than epic. For example, you could just want a new bit of content marketing for your website, and some assets to distribute it to drive traffic to it. Basically something as simple as a bit of copy, an image and a 140 character tweet would satisfy the requirements of the story. However, a 'big idea' approach would start asking in some detail what the narrative was that held the assets together, then look to produce assets for all the traditional channels like TV, press and radio that every campaign has always used, before disappearing off into a whole load of strategic research and ideation exercises in the process. In many senses, this is people reverting to their comfort zones, but it does create big risks for the scrum methodology that I shall return to later. Once again, it also highlights how important an agile mindset and culture is when implementing an agile methodology. For those with an agile mindset will believe and stay true to principle 10 of the agile manifesto:

"Simplicity - the art of maximizing the amount of work not done - is essential".

Those without it will see every story, no matter how small, as an epic story.

Ultimately, getting user stories right is a fine balance, and one for which I can't give you hard and fast rules. User stories are as much an art as a science, and like anything else in agile, it's often only through the process of doing them that you discover how they are best done in your organisation. Much of the exploration of user stories has to date only been conducted in the world of software development too. So whilst they clearly hold great potential for delivering excellent marketing campaigns, exactly how best to use them still needs to be trialed in many more situations yet.

However, there is one additional step to working with user stories that you may find helpful. We'll come back to the process you use for delivering user stories shortly, but one element of this process is to break the user story down into tasks. This involves taking a 'As a...I want to...so I can' user story and working out what the different tasks are that will need to be completed in order to deliver an output that answers the user story. At one level, this can be useful. If we take social media content as our example again, you might need a task for writing the copy, another for designing how it will look on the social media platform, another for search engine optimising it, and some others for creating the different assets you will use to distribute it once published. However, the risk with this approach is that you again end up back in your 'big idea' approach to project management.

It is not too much of a leap from 'task' into 'deliverable', so if you're not careful, you can end up specifying exactly what you will produce, rather than discovering the best thing to produce through the process of producing it. The trick is to keep the task descriptive yet vague. There is a world of difference between 'source the most appropriate image to go with the Facebook post' and 'source an image of our brand logo 720px wide to go with the Facebook post'. The former is a task that allows you to discover as you do the work, the latter is a fixed deliverable, planned up front.

In my experience, the whole 'user stories into tasks' debate is one of the many debates in agile that is not yet settled, especially within marketing. I've worked on some agile projects where the team delivering the project have screamed blue murder if you try to encourage them break stories down into tasks. 'Just give us the story' they say 'and we'll give you the best thing that answers the story'. Other teams appear completely lost if you just give them a story. 'But what do we do?' they cry, 'How do we know what we're meant to be doing if all you give us is a three line story?'.

Equally, some practitioners are currently arguing that the whole idea of a user story is wrong, and should be replaced with a 'job story' that removes the persona of the user, the 'As a...' section, and replaces it with 'When I...', in order to focus more on the motivation than the person holding the motivation [40]. Now this is still very much in the world of software development rather than

[40] For more discussion around this, see https://medium.com/the-job-to-be-done/replacing-the-user-story-with-the-job-story-af7cdee10c27

agile marketing, and more research would be needed to see if it was an appropriate departure for the creation of marketing assets specifically. Still, it just goes to show how the whole world of agile and scrum is still being explored, being tested and being evolved as a result.

As mentioned above though, the whole tasks vs. deliverables debate tends to be a function of the degree to which the project team understands the scrum process and has an agile mindset. For teams just getting to grips with it, breaking stories into tasks is possibly the best approach, as you wean them off a planned approach with specified deliverables. You need to be careful though that you don't appease their 'big idea' mindset too greatly, and write so many tasks, or tasks that slip into being deliverables, that the team is left no room for creativity and working through the different options to find the ones that might best answer the overall user story before testing them out. In my opinion, the more you can stay true to working with just user stories, and stay away from tasks and their associated risk of slipping into specifying deliverables, the better.

Following on from the topic of tasks, and the risk of them turning into deliverables, is another aspect of user stories that can risk dragging you back into the world of PRINCE2, Waterfall, time and cost. This issue centres around the issue of estimation, the process of calculating how long each task or story will take to deliver, and using these estimates to calculate when the campaign, or at least different parts of it, will be delivered. Now, I should first mention that there are some working in the fields of agile and scrum who swear blind that any attempt to estimate work and use the estimations to calculate delivery dates is tantamount to demonic heresy. Time and cost can never, ever be estimated they say, as if you estimate them, then you to some degree fix them, meaning you start flexing the quality of your deliverables, which they insist is *A Very Bad Thing*.

However, no matter how vehement such people become about this, they do not represent the settled consensus on the matter. Many others believe you can indeed estimate work and delivery dates using agile and scrum, and to a greater extent I agree with them. The clever way they do this, estimating without fixing anything absolutely, is by using something called story points. There are different ways of calculating story points, but the simplest for now is to estimate whether a story or a task is a small, medium or large piece of work. This is not to say that a small piece of work always take X hours, a medium piece Y hours and a large piece Z hours. That would be far too specific, and largely unknowable anyway if you're discovering exactly what the work is you need to do only through the process of doing it.

Instead, you allocate a story point to your estimations of whether a piece of work is small, medium or large. For the sake of this example, let us say that a small piece is worth one point, a medium piece two points and a large piece three points [41]. When working out what stories or tasks you will work on in the sprint, you estimate whether each one is a small, medium or large piece of work, assign the relevant points value to it, and then add up the total number of points in that sprint. At the end of the sprint, you can then see how many points you actually got through, and call that the velocity for the sprint. As you then run a number of sprints, you can start to judge how many points the team can deliver in each sprint, judge how many points there are in the user stories that are left to be delivered, and so work out by when you're likely to deliver them all. So individually, each estimation of a story point is

[41] It's worth saying that some scrum teams move beyond one, two or three points, and start giving items points on a much higher scale, 6, 12, 24, or using a Fibonacci sequence to determine the points available. I'll not concern you with such things here, but Google 'Story Points' if you want to do some further reading on the issue, and read some great vehement agile arguments that are perfect examples of Sayre's Law at the same time.

vague, but when story points are aggregated together and used over time, you can actually build a pretty good picture of the pace at which you're delivering things.
Speaking of pace, story points also have the benefit of helping to achieve principle eight of the agile manifesto, which states;

"Agile processes promote sustainable development. The sponsors, developers, and users should be able to maintain a constant pace indefinitely".

If you know that the team typically gets through 20 story points in a sprint, then trying to get them to deliver 40 points in one sprint will be to work them twice as hard, disrupting the constant pace and so making the process less likely to be sustainable.

However, as with tasks, there is of course a big risk in story points, one that comes to pass quite often. In the hands of an inexperienced practitioner, or one who follows agile methodologies but has not adopted an agile mindset, story points are a mere hop, skip and a jump away from detailed estimation of the work to be done, estimations that they then use to micro-manage the team. When the delivery timetable calculated from the story points starts to slip, the temptation is to berate the team for not staying true to the estimations of time and cost they would normally be required to stick to in the world of traditional project management. This of course goes against principle five of the agile manifesto, which states:

"Give (the team) the environment and support they need, and trust them to get the job done."

Just as bad, people sometimes waste time carefully documenting the story points, the sprint velocities and all sorts of other comprehensive documentation, rather than focusing on working outputs, breaking the second line of the manifesto itself.

I have to confess, this habit is one which I have been guilty of over the years. Of all the things agile aims to change, the one people find hardest to deal with is its tendency to do away with absolutely inflexible delivery dates. Not only are delivery dates a common part of our everyday language, and a common expectation of a marketing campaign, they often come with commercial realities attached. A Christmas marketing campaign can't be delivered in February. A project can't keep running past the time at which the funding ran out, and if funding runs out before the campaign is delivered, marketers can lose their jobs and marketing agencies can lose whole accounts. Not having delivery dates makes people very nervous indeed. As a result, for all it risks damaging agility, the temptation to use story points for monitoring the progress of a campaign's delivery is undeniably huge. We're brought up in a world where sticking to time and budget is ingrained into us as a good thing, so we prioritise those two factors in favour of agility, and in the end risk losing all three. Delivering late, running over budget and doing it all in a non-agile way.

It is for this reason that I'm still skeptical of introducing story points into scrum teams who are brand new to the world of agile and scrum. They're often no more than vaguely interesting anyway, and their benefit is often outweighed by the risks of giving people a ghost of their old world to cling desperately onto; estimating, documenting, planning and micro-managing, dragging the whole team away from the new agile culture they need to embrace. I really like Mike Cohn's recommendation in this area, that estimating with story points is only worthwhile when you will actually gain something from or do something worthwhile with the estimation [42].

---

[42] For more fantastic agile words of wisdom from Mike Cohn and others, check out the video training guides at https://www.frontrowagile.com/courses

Finally, there is the question as to the remit or scope of your user stories. Say you do marketing for a large organisation, full of the bureaucracy and approval processes that typically find fertile ground in organisations of significant size and age. Your current marketing approach will most probably be designed around the big idea, and possibly because of this, a number of different people will be wanting to get involved in the creation of marketing assets. I have theories about why this happens, but admittedly little proof for the theories at this stage. I suspect that each big idea, being big, leaves echoes and ripples in its wake as it moves through an organisation. For example, that campaign you did alongside the big product launch may have had such a big idea at its heart that it reshaped the brand identity at the same time, updating the logo, the tone of voice and all the rest. It may have taken the brand into unknown market territories, meaning a lawyer had to get involved to make sure no-one got sued or lost the company significant amounts of money. Perhaps an up and coming senior marketer delivered the big campaign and got a promotion out of it, meaning they're now the marketing director in charge, and like all generals, they're still fighting the last battle they fought, regardless of how the battlefield has changed. Whatever battle they're fighting, they still see themselves as the general in charge, and are unlikely to get out of your way any time soon.

All of this combines to mean that the marketing activity you're delivering has to be reviewed, critiqued and ultimately approved by a large number of people across the organisation, adding a significant amount of overhead to your campaign delivery, and risking reducing your agility. How then do you account for this problem using a scrum methodology? Well, one way would be to write user stories to cover the things internal customers or stakeholders want doing too, and work through them in your sprints. The attraction of this is that you're being open and honest about the amount of additional work these people are creating, and not trying to absorb it into some mythical project time you don't have. If you record it in this way, you also have a means of controlling these peoples' involvement, making sure they don't randomly crash into your project and knock it off course. It might be a tough conversation for a product owner to have with their director, to tell them that their request to review and personally critique each marketing asset is fine, but that it will be captured as a user story, added to the backlog and then compared with the other stories in order to take a judgment as to whether it delivers sufficient business value to be added to the next sprint, but it's certainly a conversation that could validly be had in an agile process. Indeed, I'd say it's one that really should be had.

However, this logging and evaluating a story for each element of stakeholder involvement doesn't feel like the simplest approach that could be taken, and nor is it one that maximises the amount of work not done. If all their involvement entails is regularly reviewing the assets the scrum process is producing, then it is far simpler to include them in the part of the sprint process relevant to their interests. For example, if they want to make sure that the sprints are producing assets that are in line with the wider brand story and other marketing campaigns, then invite them to the story time meeting set out below. If all they want to do is review and approve the assets once they have been created, then invite them to the sprint review meetings. If these people are still hooked on 'big idea' marketing, then chances are they'll feel happier knowing there's a formal meeting they can attend on a regular basis to keep an eye on things. How you then manage them at that meeting, well, reader, that's up to you.

The Scrum Board

Once you've got a number of exciting, juicy user stories for your marketing campaign, you're going to need somewhere to keep them. The place for this is called the product backlog, which is essentially a big list of all the user stories, all in one place. This list isn't just random though, as items in the product backlog are listed in priority order, with the product owner responsible for the prioritisation. The user stories that the product owner deems the most important ones to be working on next sit at the top of the list, and the stories decrease in priority as you move down the list. This way, it's clear what the focus and priorities of the different sprints are likely to be, although this can of course change as the project progresses.

However, user stories don't just live in a product backlog. When you select the user stories to work on in a sprint, they need to go somewhere else in order for people to work on them collaboratively. This is where the scrum board comes in.

The scrum board is very similar to a concept taken from the Toyota Way called a kanban board, which was itself inspired by Toyota engineers noticing how some companies used visual systems for working out what to order next from their suppliers. The word kanban means 'visual signal' or 'card' in Japanese, and these definitions sum up nicely what a Kanban board, and indeed a scrum board, is and what it looks like.

The most common, and some would say preferable, form of scrum board is essentially a portable whiteboard with some coloured insulating tape and Post-it notes. You take the whiteboard, mark off some columns on it with the insulating tape, and stick Post-it notes on it, each with a task or user story written on it. It ends up looking something like this.

Sprint Backlog	In Progress	Blocked	In QA	Done
Story 6	Story 4	Story 3	Story 1	Story 2
Story 7	Story 5			
Story 8				

Now the specifics of what you call the columns on a scrum board can vary quite a lot between different scrum teams, and the important thing is to find the one that works for you. I typically use the headings above, as I find them a nice representation of the different stages a user story goes through when a team is working on it. Initially, once you've chosen the top priority stories from your product backlog to go into your sprint, you put them all, either the stories or their tasks, into the 'Sprint Backlog' column. When a member of the team starts working on a story or task, they move the post-it note over to the 'In Progress' column. If at any point a story gets blocked by something, for example a lack of required information or an external dependency[43], then the card gets moved into the 'Blocked' column so everyone, especially the scrum master, can see that it is blocked. Once it's unblocked, it goes back into the 'In Progress' column, until such time as the person working on it considers it finished, when they put it in the QA column, QA being short for Quality Assurance, basically checking

[43] External dependency is often a polite way of referring to someone who doesn't understand agile that crashes into your project and metaphorically kicks the furniture around the room.

the story has been answered by the thing that's been produced. How this is done in a marketing environment is actually one of the big points of difference between scrum in a marketing context and scrum in a software development context. We shall return to this issue shortly. Once the QA process has been completed and the output answering the story has been agreed to have passed, it moves into the 'Done' column. It then stays there until the sprint review meeting, when it can finally be removed and celebrated[44].

One of the main points of a scrum board is that it is a visual thing, a thing everyone involved can look at with a glance and see what work's going on where. If you think about it, it's a very simple and sensible approach for any style of project management, but I'm always surprised how absent it remains outside of the software development world, even in organisations claiming to do agile. Being a visual thing, it's also the thing everyone gathers around during the Daly Standup meeting. Incidentally, it's better that the scrum board is a physical board, as that implies the team are all located together near it, meaning the team can meet principle six of the agile manifesto; that;

> *"The most efficient and effective method of conveying information to and within a development team is face-to-face conversation."*

However, recognising the reality of distributed scrum teams in some contexts, there are also lots of online platforms you can use for implementing the scrum methodology, all of which will provide you with the ability to produce a nice product backlog and scrum board that you can populate with user stories[45].

---

[44] Some scrum teams never throw away cards after they're done, but instead build them up in a big satisfying pile on or near the scrum board, helping the team feel like they're making progress even further. In contrast, other teams have been known to rip up cards that are done and throw them dramatically in the bin, gaining closure on a card that caused them much pain, and communicating to the rest of the team how just troublesome that card was.

Having touched then on some of the components and tools of the sprint cycle within the scrum methodology, let's look next in more detail at how that cycle runs, and the components that make it what it is.

The Sprint

In the scrum methodology, all of the actual work lives within a process called a sprint. Personally, I've never much liked this name, as it implies speed, stress and eventual exhaustion, rather than the steady and consistent delivery of work with no team burnout that agile as a philosophy promotes. If like me you think this name is a bit odd, then another term you could use is the far more neutral 'iteration'. However, for the purposes of this book, we shall refer to them as sprints.

Sprints then are cycles of work done to answer user stories, of varying but typically short lengths of time. Some sprints can run for a week, some run for three weeks, but typically my rule of thumb is to run them for two weeks. Regardless of their length, the important things to bear in mind are that each sprint contains a regular cycle of meetings or events[46], and at the end of every sprint there should be something to show for the work done. This last point is hugely important, and I shall return to it later.

So then, say our sprint will last for two weeks, what should we be doing in that time? In short, there are five key meetings or types of meeting.

---

45 I quite like https://trello.com for beginners, whilst https://www.atlassian.com/software/jira, http://www.agilezen.com and https://kanbanflow.com are great for those ready to get a bit further into agile and scrum.

46 Some people call them ceremonies, but I've never been much of a fan of that, so I shan't. Funerals are ceremonies, weddings are ceremonies, graduations are ceremonies, and they're all rather formal stilted affairs. Good sprint meetings are none of these things to my mind.

Sprint Planning

Sprint planning is the meeting that starts each individual sprint cycle. It's attended by the sprint team and the product owner, and facilitated by the scrum master. In it, the product owner runs through the list of user stories they want the team to deliver in the next sprint cycle, and agrees them with the team. It's worth saying here that the power to decide which stories are the priorities to work on in the next sprint cycle rests with the product owner and the product owner alone. However it would be a pretty non-collaborative and non-agile product owner that would be entirely deaf to the cries of the wider team if they felt the product owner were getting something drastically wrong in their choices.

Equally though, it is only the product owner that has a true sense of which stories are of most value to the business, and the risk with too much team involvement in selecting stories for the sprint is that team members' personal biases creep in too far. For instance, perhaps there's something a particular team member really, really wants to work on so they can learn a new skill, or because they personally think it's the most important thing for the business. These things are interesting to note, but I've seen scrum teams frozen into paralysis before now when the product owner has attempted to be too democratic about prioritising stories. Ultimately the business needs to stay in business in order for the scrum process to continue at all, and the product owner should never forget that. Decisions about business value and the top stories that deliver that value are ultimately the product owner's call, no one else's.

As mentioned above, the sprint planning meeting may also break down stories into smaller tasks that can be delivered in the sprint. I must stress again here though that tasks are not the same as deliverables. A task may be 'write the copy for the website' or 'design the email we will use to promote the content produced by this sprint'. They should never get into detail about what the copy should be, or what the email should look like. Those are things the team should work out during the sprint in the process of doing the work.

Whether you put whole stories or a series of tasks per story into your sprint backlog, if you want to allocate points to each of the cards you're putting into the sprint, then sprint planning is the time to do it. As covered on above, points are a non-scientific method of estimating the size of the work, that often ends up producing some quite reliable information. The way it works is this.

For each card put into the sprint, everyone at the sprint planning meeting gets to say whether they think the item on the card is a small, medium or large piece of work. This can be strange for people not used to agile or scrum, as surely the person in the room with the most expertise in answering the story on the card should be the one to make that judgment? For example, if the item on the card is likely to be answered through copywriting, then shouldn't the copywriter alone say how much work it is, rather than the graphic designer and website coder having an equal say? In short, no they shouldn't, and there are two good reasons for this.

First, letting everyone estimate the number of points for a task or story massively increases team collaboration. If the copywriter thinks the item is a large piece of work, and the graphic designer thinks it's a small piece, then immediately they can have that conversation and understand where each other is coming from. Second, it helps flag dependencies between different people's work in the team. The copywriter may think it large because they have a large amount of copy to write, and the designer's only got to lay it out on a page. However, if the copywriter had thought the task small, but the designer thought it was large, then immediately there's an interesting conversation and sharing of knowledge to be had. It may be a small amount of copy, but maybe the designer knows how difficult it will be to integrate that copy into its intended channel. Now both of them are aware of this, the designer can work more collaboratively with the copywriter early on to come up with the best solution.

The more the team collectively agrees the scale of the work, the more it can work collaboratively on getting it delivered, never getting caught up in mental distress about why one person seems to be flying through their cards, whilst they're still on their first one halfway through the sprint. You've all discussed how hard or easy your work is, so you get fewer troublesome misunderstandings around who is and isn't pulling their weight. As mentioned above, in agile you trust your team to get the job done, so discussing the scale of each card collectively at the start of a sprint helps the team trust one another far more. However, in all of these discussions, the opportunity for personal bias to creep in arises again. People can be swayed by strong personalities in the room, or by what appears to be a majority consensus, meaning they keep potentially useful information to themselves rather than sharing it with the team.

To get around this, you can use a technique called planning poker. Rather than going round the table asking people in turn for their points estimation, each person selects a card with their chosen points number written on, and all reveal their cards at the same time. This way people aren't swayed by the estimations spoken by people before them, and can be more honest about what they believe the points to be. People with high and low estimations are then asked to speak, and the issue thrashed out until an agreement is reached[47]. If an agreement can't be reached, the story goes back into the product backlog, as the lack of agreement shows that it

[47] Or, in some cases, until the time allotted for estimating that story runs out. It all depends how much your team like talking.

clearly needs further work and refinement before it can be progressed.
Once agreed, the points for each item are written on the Post-it note / card for it, so during the sprint each team member can see how difficult a task each other member of the team is likely to be having. Again, communication promotes collaboration.

Daily Standups

Once you've held your sprint planning meeting, you can get cracking with the work to start answering the user stories. The focus in agile is on getting stuff done, getting marketing assets out there, so once you know what stories you're working on, why waste any more time?

Once you've started though, there is one meeting you all need to attend every day, called the stand up. Now, this isn't just a clever name, as the meeting does exactly what it says it says on the tin. Once per day, usually at the start of the day, the entire team gathers together and has a meeting whilst standing up. This isn't some tech geek affectation, the logic behind it is quite simple. If you have a meeting whilst sitting down, it's very easy to get comfy, get some coffee in and have a bit of a chat whilst you're at it. If you have a meeting standing up, you can't do any of these things, and the meeting is an awful lot shorter as a result. Again, maximising the amount of work not done.

The standup can happen anywhere, but typically it happens around the scrum board for the sprint being worked on. This allows the team to see each item being discussed, understand where it's at in the process and how it fits in with everything else going on. Whilst in theory anyone can move a ticket they're responsible for across the different columns of the scrum board, some teams choose to move tickets only during the stand up meeting each day, in order to show more clearly to others the progress they're making or blockers they're experiencing.

At a standup meeting, the agenda is clearly fixed too. You go round each person in the team, and they say what they worked on yesterday, what they're working on today, and whether they have any blockers. Nothing more, nothing less. If anyone starts explaining what they've been doing in too much detail, or someone else asks them a question about it, the rest of the team is entirely at liberty to (cheerfully) shout 'Detail!' at them until they shut up. Now, on the face of it, this looks like a habit that reduces inter-team communication and collaboration, but actually it increases it.

Think about meetings you've been to where two or three people have dominated the room. Effectively, these few people end up having the meeting whilst everyone else in the room zones out. If stand-ups turn into detailed conversations about something specific, but not especially relevant to other people in the team, then people start zoning out, even wandering about, and overall losing focus. Instead, think of the daily standup as a way of sparking more and better inter-team communications. If anyone does pick up someone saying something they'd like to discuss further, then encourage them to have a proper detailed conversation about it after the meeting, a far more effective approach that keeps things simple for everyone else.

It's also important for each person in the stand up to say if they have any blockers or not, as the scrum master will be at the meeting, and it's their job to unblock any blockers that emerge on behalf of the team. It also helps flag if anyone in the team is blocking anyone else's work, again allowing them to notice this fact and discuss it in more detail after the stand up. Overall, the point of the daily standup in this regard is to prevent unpleasant surprises turning into nasty surprise. An unpleasant surprise is finding out that someone wasn't able to get anything done yesterday. A nasty surprise is finding out that someone hasn't been able to get their work done for the entirety of the last two weeks the sprint was running.

In short, a stand up meeting should be an energising, exciting meeting that once concluded dissolves into numerous different conversations amongst the team that have been sparked by the deceptively simple format of the meeting. If you put all of this together, the standing up, the three short things each person has to say and the collective understanding of where the sprint is up to each day, then you don't end up with a very long meeting. If you're at the sort of organisation or working with the types of marketers that require time to be booked in their diary in advance, then as a rule of thumb I'd allow 15 minutes for your daily stand up meeting. However, I generally see 15 minutes as a target to undershoot, and if the meeting lasts just five minutes, so be it. Far better to keep the meeting short and allow more time for conversations afterwards than drag it on, lose focus and leave everyone feeling a bit bored and demoralised.

Storytime

In my experience, if there's one meeting that's neglected in the scrum process, it's storytime. The idea behind storytime is to get the team together once during the sprint, often halfway through, and collectively review the stories in the main product backlog. Possibly just some of the highest value stories, possibly all of them, it depends how many stories are in your backlog at the time. Overall though, the point of it is to build in a regular time to look back at the rest of the stories that may get worked on in future, and take the opportunity to refine the product backlog stories based on what is now known. Through this process, the team questions whether the stories in the backlog still make sense or are too epic, perhaps putting some rough story points against backlog stories, and generally leaving the product backlog in better shape than when the meeting started. The additional bonus is that the team have collectively had another chance to discuss the work, share information and collaborate.

However, there are a number of reasons why storytime is so often skipped over in a sprint cycle. First, it takes time away from delivering the stories in the current sprint. If the stories in the current sprint are the most important things to be working on right now, then why take time away from them to consider stories of much lesser importance? Also, it's easy to skip over storytime and just try to do a smaller version of it in the sprint planning meeting itself. After all, if sprint planning requires you to go through stories in detail and consider the work to be done to answer them, then surely you can do the refining and improving work on the stories as part of that?

However, as much as storytime is indeed yet another meeting in everyone's diaries, deciding to miss it out really can be a false economy. It's a meeting that keeps the team's eyes on the broader project they're working on at a time when they're eyes down working on some of the detail, and it further promotes collaboration and information sharing. It also makes sprint planning meetings so much easier, as prioritised stories arrive into them well understood and simpler to work on. Indeed, if you don't use storytime to uncover some of the information you'll need to deliver the story in the sprint, you'll likely just end up using time in the sprint itself to do this work anyway. Far better to get this work fully understood and done ahead of time, than try to cram it all into the sprint.

Now naturally, in the process of working on the stories in the sprint, new needs for information will crop up. No storytime can capture everything that you need to know, as it's often only by doing the work that you find out what everything you need to know actually is. However, the more you can take this overhead out of the sprint, the more and better the exploration you'll be able to do in the sprint itself. Of course, like any meeting done badly, taking time out of a sprint for a storytime session can just feel like another overhead, a time thief that no-one would miss if it didn't exist. My advice though would be to try it, stay focused on the value it can add if done right, and then see how much value it does add to your sprints. I'd wager it adds far more value than you expect.

Sprint Review

At the end of the sprint, there comes a sprint review session. As with most things in scrum and agile, there are a few different ways of running them. The basic point of the sprint review is to gather the team together, ideally along with some people external to the team, and collectively review what has been produced in the sprint. It's a chance to get everyone together to look at and discuss what's been created. Now, how you define these people and define their roles in the meeting is where things get more complex. In some sprint reviews, the team doing the work presents their work to the product owner, who then acts as the voice of the customer in agreeing that the outputs answer the stories. In others, customers themselves are invited along, and the outputs are presented by the team, or the product owner, or just the people in the room in general. It's another opportunity for people to gather together, communicate with each other collaboratively and review the work that has been produced.

Taking this into a marketing context, I see the sprint review as a chance for external stakeholders in the marketing campaign to have their say on what it being produced, and give the team feedback that can influence their future work. Now of course the risk here is that this provides ample opportunities for people to bring a whole shed load of 'big idea' mindset into the project. After all, this is their chance to offer their personal opinion and shape the marketing assets the way they've always done and the way they believe to be right. In my opinion, it only takes a few sprint reviews like this to kill your scrum process stone dead.

As a result, unless you're working in an organisation that understands and supports agile across the board, then I think it's important for sprint reviews to be reasonably tightly controlled by the scrum master facilitating the meeting. One technique for this is to state that the purpose of the review is to compare each piece of output with the story it is intended to answer, and have attendees only comment on whether the output answers the story. Not whether they think it's the best asset ever produced, or whether they think the proposed A / B test of two different assets is pointless because the answer is clearly A, or whether they think the sprint should have been producing something completely different. After all, you've done so much work up to this point to make your customers the main focus of your marketing output, and to get away from personal bias, heavy up-front planning and 'big idea' marketing, so don't let external people come in and tell you you're doing it wrong. The people who should be telling you whether you're doing it right or wrong are your customers or end consumers, so stay focused on that. It's also worth reminding attendees that you're using agile to explore unknown marketing terrain, so you have to let the process do that, rather than reverting back to old approaches that may no longer be as relevant.

This is not to say you shut attendees up entirely, far from it. Doing so would in fact be quite ironic, as if you try to reduce discussion and collaboration to prevent them from dragging you back to the old way of doing things, you're inadvertently letting them drag you back there anyway. Besides, they can potentially add huge amounts of value to your work by using their external perspectives and access to information to let you know about new potential user stories to put into future sprints. Often this may arrive as a request to produce something for them, or change something to adapt to the reality they have observed, but with your new agile mindset, this is something you should welcome. It is also something you should make sure doesn't either get lost, so make sure to record it as a new user story and put it in the product backlog to be prioritised by the product owner later.

Here, it is worth bearing in mind that people bringing valuable external perspectives or information will likely want to prioritise their requirements over those of others, so the product owner should feel free at this point to remain firm, record their story in the backlog, and assure them that it will be prioritised by them in relation to all the other stories in the backlog. The product owner retains the overview of all of the stories that could be worked on, so only they can prioritise them fairly across multiple different, potentially competing, external viewpoints.

As the team and external parties go through each story from the sprint during the sprint review, it can be good to move each completed story into the done column, so you can immediately see at the end of the meeting how much you got done and celebrate that fact. But what about stories you don't get completed in the sprint? Ideally there shouldn't be any, as once you get a sense of how much the team can deliver at a sustainable pace in a sprint, each sprint can be set up to contain just that amount of work. However, the reality can sometimes be different, and you find yourself with incomplete tasks or stories at the end of a sprint.

The important thing to remember here is that unfinished stories or tasks don't just automatically get carried over to be worked on in the next sprint. There are a few reasons for this. First, if you automatically carry stories over, then you're effectively negating the point of sprinting at all. If the project becomes one steady flow of work, each piece being worked on until it is finished, no matter how long this takes, then dividing the project into sprints becomes pointless. Now, there are a good number of agile practitioners who see this as no bad thing. If sprints aren't adding any value, and you can produce just as much output, if not more, through dispensing with them and their formalities, then why bother with time-boxed sprints at all?

Whilst I have some sympathy with this view, I think it's potentially short-sighted. For example, if a story is proving particularly troublesome, if not impossible, then do you really want the team to continue to work on it? You only truly learn how difficult something is or isn't in agile through the process of doing it, so no matter how many storytimes and careful sprint planning sessions you've done, it's perfectly possible that you've taken on a story which turns out to cost far more to deliver than the value it will return, or even just can't be delivered at all. Equally, perhaps new information has come to light since you started work on the story, which has shown that the story no longer has as much value as it did when you started. This is perfectly possible when you're working in complex, fast-paced and uncertain environments. In any event, automatically returning every unfinished story into the product backlog at the end of every sprint review forces you to consider possibilities like these. It may be that the story isn't actually problematic, and still has high value, or will cost very little more to complete. In which case feel free to take it straight back out of the backlog and put it in the next sprint. However, always do this consciously, not automatically.

Finally, sprint planning shows the value of one of the most important aspects of an agile project. As principle seven of the agile manifesto states:

> *"Working software is the primary measure of progress."*

Replace 'working software is' with 'publishable marketing assets are' and you get the idea. If you have nothing to show in your sprint review, then you clearly have an issue in your project that you need to resolve. It may of course be that what the sprint has produced looks nothing like people thought it would produce, and often such things will be better than the original expectations. However, if the sprint isn't producing anything at all, then that's something to worry about. Sprint review thus has another use in keeping the team's eye on this question too, one that may be missed if you just run one long sprint without beginning or end.

Retrospective

Finally, at the end of every sprint comes the retrospective meeting. This is often run straight after the sprint review meeting, but if it is, you need to tell all external people to clear off, as this is a meeting for the scrum master, product owner and team members only. The retrospective meeting is an opportunity for the core project team to reflect on how the work went over the last sprint. What worked well? What didn't work so well? What could they agree to do differently over the next sprint in order to work together even better?

Retrospectives are another area in which agile marketing wins big over 'big idea' marketing. In 'big idea' approaches, you spend weeks and months planning every aspect of the campaign and creating all the assets, before launching them all in a big bang approach. However, how often during this process do you take time to stop and think about how well your process is working, and how you could make it even better? Not often I'd wager. Indeed, sometimes campaigns conclude without any look back at what went well and what went badly at all.

In contrast, in scrum, you do this at the end of every sprint, so you're constantly improving how you work together. It is another reason why I'm surprised when people get too hung up on the rights and wrongs of agile and scrum. The process has got to work for the team, and work within the environment in which it is operating, an environment that may very well change as the project progresses. Even if the environment doesn't change, there may be changes in the way the project needs to work based on new information the team has uncovered.

As a result, a retrospective meeting is a really important part of the sprint process, but it's not so important as to warrant a lot of time and agonising over. You'll have another one in a couple of weeks or so at the end of the next sprint, and another at the end of the sprint after that, so you don't need to work out how to get to perfection in every retrospective. Instead, keep the retrospective snappy, to the point, and with clear and simple actions around how the team will change and optimise its ways of working over the next two weeks. I also feel that the more retrospectives get bogged down in detailed discussion, the more they risk losing sight of the bigger picture.

Agile processes aren't about performance metrics, speed and in-depth quantitative evaluation. They're about collaboration, communication and many other human inter-personal relationships. As a result, I often think it's also good to discuss things like feelings and worries in a retrospective meeting. If someone's feeling the current process is overwhelming them or frustrating them, far better to talk it through as a collaborative team than let the person sit there stewing and being less productive over the coming sprints. Obviously, the degree to which you get all touchy-feely with a retrospective meeting is up to you. They're not group therapy sessions after all. But using retrospectives to keep an eye on the human elements of your marketing and communications process is, I believe, a really important benefit of keeping them in your sprint diary.

Dramatis Personae

So we've talked about the stories, scrum board, sprint cycle and ceremonies contained within the agile methodology of scrum.

However, though all of this discussion, various different job titles have kept cropping up, none of which I have yet explained. Scrum has a number of different specific roles for members of the team to play, and a number of different practices for them to carry out. So then, who are the people that work on your scrum based project? There are four key types of people in scrum; the product owner, the scrum master, team members and customers. Let's go through each of them in turn to find out what they do.

The Product Owner

When I give presentations about agile and scrum, I generally use a photo of Martin Luther King Jr. to represent the product owner. For in scrum, a good product owner really is a visionary and leading figure. First, scrum accepts that if progress is to be made and options are to be explored, then you can't let everyone make every decision. The more people you add to a decision making process, the longer it takes. Besides, if you're responding to change rather than following a plan, why take up a lot of different people's time in planning and deliberation when you could just be finding the best approach through rapidly prototyping different options and testing them out as quickly as possible in the external marketing environment?

However, just as we saw in chapter two above, having a team work randomly on different ideas would be to work on your marketing in the absence of any intention towards an end goal, a practice as unlikely and potentially harmful as the purely deliberate approach which sits at the opposite extreme. In short, if you don't want constant decision making by committee, and all of the personal opinions and biases such practices inevitably contain, someone's got to be around to take the calls on which directions to take as the marketing materials get worked up. This person is the product owner.

The product owner in scrum has a number of different roles, all related to the central idea of them being the unifying figure that leads and guides the project as it goes along. During the sprint, the product owner acts as the customer to the rest of the team. If and when the team come up against a decision that has to be made about the direction of the work, it's the product owner's job to be available to answer questions at any time, and represent the customer in the decisions they make.

The product owner's role is not limited to guiding the work during the sprint though. They're also responsible for recording user stories and maintaining the backlog of user stories that the team could work on in future sprints. More important, they're also responsible for prioritising this backlog of user stories; identifying those which hold the greatest value to the business and making sure they get worked on next. The product owner is there to maximize the value of the work to the business using the scrum methodology.

However, it is important to recognize the boundaries of the product owner's responsibilities. As we have touched on already, it is team members who are responsible for how they get their work done. The product owner is not there to project manage the team, or use the scrum tools in order to performance manage any individuals within the team. This is a bit of a departure from how project managers normally operate in delivery processes, but it entirely accords with some of the principles of agile manifesto. Principle five of the agile manifesto states:

> *"Build projects around motivated individuals. Give them the environment and support they need, and trust them to get the job done."*

Likewise principle 11 states;

"The best architectures, requirements, and designs emerge from self-organizing teams."

If the product owner steps over their line of responsibility into performance management or micro-management, then they're essentially sending a clear signal that they don't trust the team or don't want them to self-organise. This inevitably reduces their motivation, and quite possibly motivates them to self-organize away from the project and onto another one with a better product owner.

The product owner is a tricky role to fill. On the one hand they've got a significant amount of power and influence over whether the project is a success or failure. On the other hand, they often have to bite their tongue and trust the team not to let them down. Responsibility without control is an uncomfortable place to sit at times, so a product owner really does need to have adopted an agile mindset at quite a deep level, believing in collaboration, welcoming change and trusting in the team to get the work done to the best of their ability.

The Scrum Master

If agile is unique in not having a project manager in the traditional sense, it is the role of the scrum master that makes it even more unique. A good scrum master is hugely important to the success or failure of a scrum based project, and is a role quite unlike any other in the traditional project management world.

The main job of the scrum master is to clear blockers out of the way of the team. As we've seen above in the sprint cycle, as team members work on tasks, it's quite possible that some of the tasks will get blocked. Perhaps in the process of doing the work, it turns out some more information is needed before the story can be completed. Perhaps the team haven't got all the tools they need to get the job done. Perhaps something somewhere in the wider organisation is crashing into the project and blocking the team from doing their work. It's at times like these that the team get on their batphone and bring the scrum master in to unblock their issue. Indeed, so important is this role for the scrum master, that as you'll have noticed above, one of the three things each member of the team comments on in the daily stand up is whether or not they've currently got any blockers stopping them getting work done.

This work clearing blockers is definitely not to be underestimated. If you think about it, a blocker is a problem that the team member can't fix themselves. For example, a team member may be blocked from working by the fact that their computer is turned off. So to clear the blocker, all they have to do is turn the computer on. In contrast, if someone elsewhere in the business is failing to provide the information the team member needs in order to complete the story, then the blocker can only be cleared when the other person decides to provide the information. A good scrum master thus has to be a great political operator, skilled at getting things to happen and solving problems. Now this is not to say that scrum masters have to be managing directors of successful global management consultancies, supremely skilled at solving the knottiest problems of business in the 21st century. They do however have to be unafraid of challenging convention, able to identify areas that need to improve and able to build connections across the wider business. As in my experience, some of the biggest, most challenging and significant threats to any scrum project come from outside of the project itself, from people and processes across the wider business.

The fact I mention something from elsewhere in the business crashing into the project and causing issues is quite deliberate, as this is a very common issue, especially when only certain parts of the business are working in an agile way. In scrum, the team is meant to be working solely on the sprint, and so it's the scrum master's job to protect the team from any external interruptions. I used to see this a lot when I was working as a product owner on agile software projects, whilst also doing my day-to-day job account handling various existing customers. A customer would phone up and ask us to make a change to one of their websites. It might have been a big change, it might have been a trivial one, but either way, my account handler instincts kicked in, and I'd dash down to find a friendly developer to make the change for me a.s.a.p. However, if I did this, the scrum master would be there telling me to go away. The developers were working on a sprint, and could not be interrupted.

"*But, but, what about the client!? The client is always right!*"

I'd stutter in response, but it didn't matter. As the scrum master used to explain to me, I could either have one disappointed client right now, or many disappointed clients in two weeks time when we didn't deliver any of them the things we'd promised to deliver in that sprint. In terms of business value, the choice was a no brainer.

Of course, there is the risk that this role of scrum master becomes too important, even too self-important. Life happens, fire alarms go off, people need to eat, the result of the football match last night was so shocking that it warrants immediate discussion. Taken to its logical conclusion, a scrum master protecting the team from interruptions and removing things that stop them getting work done could fall into the same potential trap as the product owner, ruling the team and those around them with a rod of iron, rather than trusting them and working collaboratively.

As a result, the role of the scrum master is very much seen as one based on coaching, helping the team get the most out of the scrum and continually optimising the scrum process. If you know there's other non-sprint related work members of the team need to get done during the sprint, then there's no harm in collectively agreeing an afternoon for them to come off the sprint and do something else. What can cause harm though is doing these things in an ad hoc manner. Once a scrum master gives the impression that a sprint is just one of the many things the team could choose to work on at any given time, then the whole scrum process can quickly fall apart. Again, the scrum master has to be as much of a judge and politician as the product owner.

One final point to mention about the scrum master is that if they are there to coach the team in scrum and make sure they can keep getting the work done, then it's not too much of a leap of imagination to see them as a pivotal role in spreading agile across a business. We've already seen in chapter three that introducing and spreading agile is best done in an emergent manner, passed down from person to person through practical experience as much as formal learning. So to my mind, if you want to start to introduce an agile approach in your organisation, you probably need more trained scrum masters with genuine agile mindsets than any other type of person. Not to say you won't need capable product owners and team members too, but I suspect it is from hiring or training up scrum masters that you will see the most change come about and most business value demonstrated.

The Team

Whilst the product owner leads, represents the customer and maximises the business value created by the project, and the scrum master removes blockers, protects the team from distraction and coaches cohesiveness, the team are the people in scrum who actually get the work done to deliver the user stories and / or tasks during the sprint.

In the agile presentations I give, when I talk about the team, I usually use a picture of the borg from Star Trek to illustrate them. This is not to say team members in scrum are emotionless cyborgs looking to assimilate others in their quest for perfection. Although some scrum teams do feel a little like that sometimes when vehement arguments kick off about someone 'Doing Scrum Wrong'. No, I use the image of the Borg to make the point that in a scrum team, every member works collaboratively as one team, with no fixed barriers between who does which parts of the work. Of course, some people will be better skilled and better suited for some parts of the work than others, and it makes sense that they work on it. However, their area of specialism is not their domain alone, and if someone else in the team has something useful to contribute to this person's area, they should be encouraged to do so.

In a scrum based software development project, you'd have a range of skills and roles in the team. Typically you'd have a few coders writing the code for the software. Alongside them you'd have at least one user interface designer, turning the code from basic functionality into something that's easy and enjoyable for people to use. You may also have a tester, testing and quality assuring the outputs of the other team members with a fresh pair of eyes as the work progresses. If you apply scrum to marketing, the mix of roles might not actually be that different. You could have a couple of copywriters writing the copy for the marketing assets. Alongside them a designer, turning the plain old copy into something beautiful, eye catching and on brand. You may well have a quality assurance person as well, looking at what everyone's producing and checking for typos, factual errors and anything else that can go wrong. In addition, you may bring in some more specialist roles. Perhaps a search engine optimization expert, ensuring that the assets produced are going to deliver maximum bang for their buck when it comes to ranking in Google and other search engines. Maybe a user journey person as well, keeping an eye on how each of the different assets produced will hang together for the end user and not send them off into a dead end during the sales journey. You may even have a lawyer, checking your not going to get sued or sanctioned for any of your outlandish marketing claims.

Whoever you include in your scrum team, the following facts are the most important. The scrum team is the team responsible for completing the tasks to answer the user stories. They're to be trusted, allowed to self-organize and allowed to choose their own tools and techniques for getting the work done. Scrum masters and product owners are there to coach, guide and support the team, protecting it from external buffeting and helping it perform to the best of its abilities, but they are not there to micro-manage, tightly control or sanction the team if, in their judgment, it performs badly.

What goes for the product owner and scrum master also goes for the team members towards each other too. Whilst each person in the team may have specific areas of competence or responsibility, their roles are set out using the concept of boundaries rather than barriers. If you think about it, a boundary is something that you know marks the edge of something, but doesn't necessarily stop you crossing over it. A barrier on the other hand both marks the edge of something and stops you crossing over it. Boundaries are permeable and allow information and knowledge to cross over them, barriers restrict the flow of information and communications. As Chin puts it;

"In the agile environment, team members need to develop the art of crossing boundaries—not because they want to be involved or share credit for parts of the project, but because diverse contributions are valuable and needed. The agile project environment is complex in nature. It requires people to stretch beyond their traditionally defined areas of expertise to solve multidimensional problems that have never presented themselves before." [48]

---

[48] Chin, G. (2004). *Agile project management: how to succeed in the face of*

Of course, there is a risk with this idea of barriers. If anyone can start working on anything at any point, picking things up randomly, then dropping them to work on something else that catches their eye, you could pretty soon end up with chaos. I would however offer two responses to this viewpoint.

The first is that the risk of chaos is not peculiar to agile, as the barrier based approach found in big idea marketing and traditional project management can, when taken to extreme, equally cause chaos. Think of a situation where planners plan, creatives create and project managers make sure everything get delivered on time and on budget. Taken to its extremes, this approach means that each type of person starts to focus only on their work, sitting in their silo ignoring the work of others. Soon, your marketing activity starts to fragment into a number of different and independent projects, all ignoring the others around them and creating chaos as a result. Sometimes people even try to address this by introducing formal processes and procedures setting out how teams should work together. But taken to extreme, these too can cause more chaos, as if you have too many processes and too much governance to follow, no-one can remember all of it at the same time. So people start implementing different parts of it in different ways, and the processes designed to bring order to chaos just lead to even more chaos themselves.

So both scrum based and traditional project management approaches are at risk of chaos if they extend to their logical conclusion. However, scrum does have a number of elements that help reduce this risk quite significantly. We've already seen a number of these throughout this book; the way scrum promotes collaboration through regular communication in the different meetings of the sprint cycle, how it allows a product owner to set

---

changing project requirements. New York: AMACOM. p. 41.

direction and judge the business value of pieces of work, how it stops after every sprint to consider if things could be working better than they currently are.

In addition, there is one other chaos reducing factor that is particular to the people working in the scrum team as a whole. Typically, they work on the project full time. At first glance, this may sound obvious. If they're not working on the project full time, then what else are they doing with their time? What else would a marketer work on other than a marketing campaign? Well, there are two things here, and I've seen both happen in numerous different environments. The first is that the team members end up working on multiple projects at the same time. These may be different marketing campaigns, or different software builds, but in either event, one project ends up crashing into another, getting more attention than the other, or generally meaning neither project receives a team member's full attention, and invariably both end up failing. Deciding to work full time on one particular thing for a period of time is actually quite a departure from how most people normally work, and can be especially difficult if other parts of the business around the agile or scrum team still have this bad habit.

The second issue again typically comes from outside of the team, but instead of being another project, is just another overhead. We often lose track of how much of our working lives we spend filling in someone else's paperwork, or sitting in meetings that we're not sure why we've been invited to, or doing compulsory organisation-wide training courses, or any number of other distractions. Just like multiple projects, these non-project related overheads can hugely interrupt a scrum team, a problem that's compounded by the fact that scrum teams need to be so collaborative. If not all of the team are present all of the time, collaboration is massively reduced, and the project hugely suffers as a result. It is for this reason that the scrum master has the requirement to protect the team from interruptions. A task that can be hugely difficult to achieve, but is none the less hugely important.

So then, we've now spent some time considering what agile is. We've looked at why the new digital marketing landscape means that we need it, looked at how it differs from traditional 'big idea' approaches to marketing, and how we might implement its philosophy through using the scrum methodology. But having covered these basics, we must look next at some of the nuances. If agile, and even scrum to some degree, are concepts that are hard to pin down exactly, which parts of it make the most difference to your success, and which could you perhaps adapt to suit your specific circumstances?

Chapter 6 - The Factors That Matter

As we have seen throughout this book, despite, or perhaps because of the arguments and disagreements about what agile is, and how to use methodologies such as scrum to bring it to life, it's sometimes hard to give you a firm set of rules around it. On the one hand, if I get too prescriptive with a strict list of do's and don'ts, I reduce your ability to adapt the agile approach into your organisation. On the other hand, if I just give you a rough idea of what to do and leave you to get on with it, chances are your implementation of agile will stall and fall apart sooner rather than later. On top of this, let us not forget that what we are considering here is the translation of a software development philosophy and methodology into the worlds of marketing, PR and communications, all very different environments. Thus even if it were possible to give hard and fast rules about what you should do, these rules should not be given without careful consideration of exactly how they could cross over into the marketing sphere from the world of software.

So, a happy middle ground is needed, and the best way to do this is for me to talk you through some of the different factors that could be found in an implementation of agile, and consider them in greater detail. First, we should notice that agile and scrum are actually quite adaptive things. Scrum even has its own phrase for this, 'scrumbut', which is the practice of using some parts of scrum whilst leaving other parts out. This word comes from the usual way people explain this, saying:

"*We do scrum, but we don't do X, Y or Z parts of it*"

Some people argue that scrumbut is little more than avoiding and papering over a significant project issue, rather than facing and resolving the issue head on [49], and I have some sympathy with this

[49] See https://www.scrum.org/scrumbut and

view. From an organisational and cultural change perspective, if you start letting people believe that any part of the scrum practice can just be ignored if it's inconvenient, then I doubt your implementation will get very far. That said, there may be some things you just can't do at an early stage, practices that will only start to happen properly once agile and scrum have started to be embedded more fully. As a result, I'd keep the phrase scrumbut in the back of your mind, but be very careful if you do ever let it happen.

Having said that then, what factors of your agile implementation of scrum process matter, and which could be adapted to suit a marketing environment? This is obviously a part of this book that is very much a work in progress. Until more organisations start to adopt agile for their marketing, PR and communications delivery, we can only know a finite amount of things about how a software development approach transitions across into different fields. However, through my experiences in leading and coaching these sorts of transitions to date, I believe that there is quite a number of different factors at play here. Let's work through them in turn.

Self-organising teams

Principle 11 of the agile manifesto states;

"The best architectures, requirements, and designs emerge from self-organizing teams."

Now, this is an interesting principle to apply in practice, as it is possible to interpret the term 'self-organising' in various ways.

First, there is the issue of how the team comes together in the first place. Some would argue that the best agile or scrum teams are

---

http://agileatlas.org/articles/item/fractional-scrum-or-scrum-but for more.

entirely self-forming; a group of people who spontaneously decide to band together of their own accord to work on an iterative, adaptive project. Certainly teams formed in this way can achieve huge successes. Just look at the way various tech startup companies are formed. A group of people with a shared idea and vision get together, quit their day job and risk it all exploring a market proposition that has not been attempted before. There is a huge amount of similarity between startup companies, especially in the tech sector, and agile teams. These companies probably don't use the scrum methodology for running absolutely everything they do[50], but they often use it for at least some parts of their work, a field currently known as 'Lean Startup' [51]. In addition, it is interesting to note the passion and dedication found in teams that form in this way. People are all consciously choosing to work together collaboratively to explore the unknown with little guarantee of the outcome, so they have to believe passionately in what they're doing. This passion halos out into all sorts of other good stuff, from increased communication to increased collaboration and beyond.

However, if great scrum teams are only great when they are a micro version of this phenomenon, then how realistic is it to expect you to build a great scrum team in your organisation? In reality, established organisations aren't formed of people who spontaneously come together with shared goals. Instead they are formed by people who have all been through a standardised, likely non-agile, hiring process. Once hired, they are generally assigned work in a pre-planned manner by people with greater hierarchical authority. In so many ways this practice, whilst common across the marketing industry, is the antithesis of agile.

[50] Writing, refining and prioritising a user story to ensure there's always milk in the communal office fridge is probably overkill.

[51] See http://theleanstartup.com for more

So, we have to accept that in its purest sense, any shift to agile marketing and communications in an established organisation will likely not realise the full benefits of self-organising teams that startups can enjoy, at least not without radical culture change. This is not to say that this is not important, and indeed I believe that when starting to build an agile organisation, you can get pretty close to the literal sense of self-organising teams by using this simple method. Just look first for the people who understand agile and scrum, or are at least intrigued by it. Get these people together, and work out if you can put some sort of pilot project together for you all to work on. This may be done in people's spare time, or in some occasional downtime in between the routine tasks of the day job [52].

As they try their pilot out, they should be open to new people joining the team, either as participants or just observers. If the team and process excites them, they should be encouraged to go out and run their own pilots too. Once you've got a few pilots under your belt, you probably need to return to the real world and put a business case together for turning your pilots into formal projects, which if successful will in turn start to form their own agile projects. Hopefully, before you know it, agile's part of your standard approach.

The lesson from this is that collaborative, communicative agile teams can't help but welcome people into their world, or act as evangelists for an agile approach. This enthusiasm can be infectious, and before you know it, you've got the principle of self-forming teams nicely established. That said, it is not unlikely that from time to time management will slip back into their old ways and suddenly appoint people into your team, or remove people

52 I always find it interesting how energised agile practitioners in happy scrum teams are the people most likely to put in free discretionary effort outside of working hours, whilst those working in a non-agile way seem much more likely to stick strictly to the 9 to 5.

from it, especially if they lose their bottle over deadlines and delivery dates not being truly knowable. If you can't control the delivery date, then you can at least try to bring it forward by adding more people into the team right?

Well, no. There is a phenomenon known as Brooks' Law, created by Fred Brooks in the 1970's in his book called 'The Mythical Man Month' [53]. This law states that:

> *"Adding more people to a late software project makes it later."*

This seems counter-intuitive, but it happens for a number of reasons. First, each time you add someone new into the team, it takes them a while to get up to speed with where the work is at and so start working at maximum productivity. So not only will their outputs initially be less than you might estimate by looking at the rest of the existing team, the process of getting them up to speed risks the rest of the team having to take time out of productive work in order to bring the new person on board. So overall you actually make the project slower rather than quicker. In addition, the more people you add to a team, the more the overheads of inter-team communication start growing, again taking up time and reducing communication, collaboration and a lot of the other points of introducing agile in the first place. There's a reason scrum authors suggest an optimal size for a scrum team sits somewhere between five and nine people.

There is another problem that the concept of the self-organising team risks bringing upon itself, the phenomenon of people leaving the team. Of course, this can happen at any time for any number of reasons, but is likely to take two forms, short-term and long-term.

---

[53] http://www.amazon.co.uk/Mythical-Man-month-Essays-Software-Engineering/dp/0201835959/

Someone leaving the team in the short-term might be caused by something as simple as illness and sick leave, or something slightly more frustrating such as a team member getting pulled out of a sprint to work on something unrelated but very important and very urgent. Both happen, both will likely continue to happen, and so rather than being absolutist about it, we have to accommodate it. More severe, but no more impossible, is someone leaving the team permanently. This has the same immediate short-term costs as short-term absence, but also has additional downsides in terms of loss of longer term productivity, and the need to bring someone new into the team to replace them which, as we have seen, is best avoided if possible.

Here agile finds a real tension in itself, as item two of the agile manifesto states that agile prioritizes 'working software over comprehensive documentation'. Yet it is very often comprehensive documentation that allows the cumulative experience and knowledge of the team to be captured and more easily shared with others, especially those who may have to step in to replace team members. In addition, if the knowledge and experience is not recorded anywhere other than in the head of the person leaving the team, then their departure may mean the knowledge is lost for good. However, if you're discouraged from creating too much documentation, how do you make sure knowledge is not lost?

The solution, or at least mitigation, for both of these issues lies in increasing the number of people around the core team who are up to speed with agile and scrum, and are also regularly kept up to speed with the progress and thought processes of the project. If you think about it, this is a practice agile actively encourages in its promotion of collaboration and interaction between individuals. As a result, if the core team is being sufficiently collaborative throughout its work, then bringing external people into the project shouldn't take too long, as they already know the journey it's been on, where it's now at and how it is likely to structure and run itself.

Now, the risk inherent in getting this to happen is that someone sees it as so important that they start to formalise it. They force people to attend meetings other teams' meetings, checking that lots of people understand what the team is up to, and are capable of being swopped in and out of the team at a moment's notice. Perhaps they even try swopping people in and out of the team, just to check that it works. However, this situation would mean one person was effectively writing the agile process everyone has to follow, then micromanaging how they follow it, the antithesis of agile

A far better way would be to facilitate this approach rather than enforce it. People who do not hold the agile mindset or do not understand scrum are often quite toxic to scrum teams and the agile approach more generally. So the more people you can get to adopt the mindset and understand scrum, the more people you will happily be able to allow into your scrum teams as the need arises. Notice I say 'allow into' rather than 'tell to join'. If you must swop team members around, then as the saying goes, 'a volunteer is worth ten pressed men'.

Of course, there is also a far more simple solution to the problem of team self-organisation and turnover. Reduce the number of team members who end up leaving the team in the first place. It is well acknowledged that low levels of personal satisfaction and high levels of stress lead to higher staff absence through sickness and higher staff turnover, as staff look for jobs that don't make them cry. So do all you can to keep staff happy, engaged, motivated and productive. This is one of the reasons I suggested having your retrospective meeting look at interpersonal and fluffy issues such as team feelings and happiness in chapter five above. Equally, if another reason behind staff churn on a project is people getting pulled out of the project to work on other things, then this is an opportunity for the scrum master to step up to the plate and carry out their job of protecting the team from distractions.

Colocation

So, once your scrum team has been formed, once you know who they are and they don't look like they're going to go anywhere anytime soon, where do you put them? This is an issue that in my experience isn't too often considered in marketing activity. Sure, some marketing campaign teams may sit in the same office, or work together quite closely. Equally common though is a situation where some of the team involved in delivering the campaign are all client-side but still spread across different offices, whilst others are based in external agencies, or are freelancers primarily working from home.

All of these situations would make some agile practitioners twitch and gibber. Principle six of the agile manifesto states:

> *"The most efficient and effective method of conveying information to and within a development team is face-to-face conversation."*

Essentially to work in an agile way, you need to have the entire team located in the same physical space, able to talk to each other face-to-face at any time. Where this is not possible, various studies have shown agile often fails to get off the ground, or if it does, it fails to remain in flight for long [54].

The reasons for this are simple. If people are located together, it is easier for them to communicate. Speaking to the person next to you is easier than trying to get them on the phone or waiting for them to reply to an email. Not only is the process of communication easier,

---

[54] Cohn, M. & Ford, D. (2003). 'Introducing an agile Process to an Organization' *Computer, IEEE Computer Society*, pp. 74-78

the quality of the resulting communication is also higher. With face to face communication you benefit from a whole load of additional non-verbal communication, you get it at a faster rate and in a more collaborative, deliberative style. Through all of these small shared communications, you also start to develop a shared team culture. For example, people who are located together often tend to go down the pub more with each other after work, giving them a new opportunity to chew over the problems and successes of the day in a different context and perhaps a less formal style. In short, you develop a more communicative, more collaborative and higher performing team. One that shares a common understanding of the agile mindset being used and how the scrum process is in reality being implemented.

There is also the fact that non-collocated teams often increase people's nervousness about the quality and pace of the work being done. It's easier to see how much someone is getting through, and whether what they're producing is what's needed, when they're sitting next to you than when they're in a different building. When people get nervous, they risk reverting to their plan-based comfort zones by starting to exercise greater control over other team members, trusting them less and planning their activities more, in a desperate attempt to gain the visibility that would normally be so apparent if everyone sat in the same room. This sort of behaviour is of course a big risk to remaining agile and following scrum in a meaningful way. You could call it scrumbut, but as with many things in scrumbut, it's quite likely just a method of papering over a problem that should instead be resolved.

However, to get too purist about this is to deny the reality of the current marketing landscape. If you took collocation of the marketing team to its logical conclusion, all marketing and advertising agencies would cease to exist, and all campaigns would be delivered in house using a collocated team. With the WPP group alone currently turning over billions of pounds per year, this seems unlikely. So either we modify our stance on collocation, or we abandon transferring agile into the world of marketing and communications altogether.

Whilst I believe collocation of agile teams is hugely beneficial and important, and have experienced first hand agile projects come crashing down due to a lack of it, I think it is important to focus not on colocation in and of itself, but on the benefits collocation brings about. How can they be maintained in a situation where collocation is still the goal, but exceptions are allowed to exist? As we have seen, collocation is about promoting communication, collaboration, a shared culture and mutual trust amongst the team. If we can preserve those elements, does the physical location in and of itself matter?

Let's remember that since the publication of the agile manifesto in 2001, communications technology has come a long way. Skype now lets people be face-to-face quickly and simply even when they're on opposite sides of the planet. In theory, the non-collocated scrum team could sit in front of tablet computers, each dialed into Skype permanently, effectively bringing everyone face to face through technology. Equally, I have seen private IRC groups[55] used effectively for keeping the scrum team talking throughout the sprint. Indeed, IRC has the added benefit that conversations are captured in text form, meaning anyone in the team can go back and read them when they want, rather than being distracted by conversations happening face-to-face, although this is balanced by the loss of non-verbal communication. However, inter-personal communications technology is advancing all the time, and I believe that the collocation debate is another element of agile that cannot yet be fully settled in its conclusions.

[55] Instant Relay Chat. Basically those online instant messenger things you can use from Hotmail to Facebook these days.

Looking at collocation in terms of its effects rather than absolutes also allows us to avoid another trap; recognising that whilst agile may not necessarily mean collocation, collocation in its turn does not necessarily mean agile. In an unthinking implementation of an agile approach, there is the risk of thinking that you have achieved agility because all of your team work in one room. This is clearly not the case. If collocation is about communication, collaboration, a shared culture and mutual trust, then just having people in the same room doesn't necessarily mean any of these things will happen. For instance, members of the team may have argued vehemently early on in the project, they may even still be arguing now about who is implementing agile or scrum in the 'right' way. Sometimes, they may have argued so much that they are in fact no longer talking. The strong personalities which caused these arguments may also start to divide the team, forcing team members to take sides, spreading the lack of collaboration beyond just the original instigators. Even those not involved in this and remaining neutral may start to despair at the way the team is fragmenting, so whilst their bodies may still be collocated with the rest of their team members, their minds could be a million miles away. Indeed, I would argue that collocation often makes these problems worse, as you force people who hate each other to be in each other's presence day in, day out, never getting any space to themselves.

So, collocation is a double edged sword in many ways. Fundamentally, it is hugely useful and hugely important to the successful implementation of agile and scrum. However, it is not the be all and end all, it may increasingly be able to be replaced over time as technology evolves. Ultimately, it is only a good technique if it provides the benefits it promises, rather than being a universally good thing in and of itself.

Communication

Following on from this discussion of communication, and the risk of people arguing, it is worth considering not the form in which communication happens, for example whether people are collocated or not, but how to ensure that communication happens as much as possible and as well as possible. How do you ensure that knowledge is shared, ideas are discussed and a common team culture established? I think there are two aspects to this.

The first is in the nature of your team members. This is often a slightly taboo subject in the modern workplace. Discrimination laws abound, and many organisations both hire new employees and evaluate existing ones using more neutral sets of criteria, based around competencies rather than personalities. There is also the risk that if you start looking too closely at people's personalities and inter-personal behaviours, you start 'playing the man not the ball', leading people to feel criticised for who they are, fragmenting the team and killing collaboration.

However, given the way in which agile promotes and relies upon inter-personal communication, I think it is foolish to leave this issue entirely unconsidered. Authors such as Coram and Boehner suggest that members of a team based on agile principles:

> *"must be amicable, talented, skilled, and able to communicate well."* [56]

Hunter goes further, using a Myers-Briggs personality type classification to analyse the personality profiles of people working in the software development industry[57], the very people who are so

[56] Coram, M., & Bohner, S. (2005). 'The impact of agile methods on software project management', in *Proceedings of the 12th IEEE International Conference and Workshops on the Engineering of Computer-Based Systems*, pp. 363-370.
[57] Hunter, A. (2009). 'High-tech Rascality: Asperger's Syndrome, Hackers, Geeks,

often responsible for working with and popularising the agile philosophy. She finds that the typical Myers-Briggs personality profile of software developers is ISTJ, and concludes:

> *"that the computer industry has very few SF (sensing, feeling) types – friendly sympathetic people who are keen to help others."* [58]

This may be another factor that helps explain why arguments about agile have been so common over the years.

Of course, this is a difficult problem to prevent if agile teams are self-selecting and self-organising. But don't forget that coaching the team to work better together is one of the roles of the scrum master, so your project does have resource dedicated to resolving this problem if it emerges. It is also not clear, and in need of further research, whether this personality issue found in software development is likely to occur in the marketing environment. As an initial hypothesis, I'd suggest that marketers, PR people and professional communicators are inherently more outgoing and communicative people, due to the nature of their job and vocation. Perhaps this problem will look entirely different as agile becomes more mainstream within the world of marketing and communications. I look forward to finding out.

The second issue is how agile and scrum promote communication. We have looked at this elsewhere in this book, but it is worth covering here briefly too. As we saw in chapter five, the different meetings held during a sprint aren't just there because meetings are deemed to be an important thing to hold regularly. A huge part of their benefit lies in the communication they promote. For example,

---

and Personality Types in the ICT Industry', *New Zealand Sociology*, Vol. 24, No. 2, pp. 39-61.

[58] Hunter, A. (2009). 'High-tech Rascality: Asperger's Syndrome, Hackers, Geeks, and Personality Types in the ICT Industry', *New Zealand Sociology*, Vol. 24, No. 2, p. 51.

daily stand ups are deliberately short and simple so that they can spark further conversation, increasing the overall amount of communication taking place. Sprint planning and storytime sessions are an opportunity for the team to communicate with one another and develop a shared understanding of the work to be undertaken. Sprint reviews promote communication with those outside of the team, and retrospectives allow the team to communicate openly and honestly how they think the work is going. These are simple facts, but all to easily forgotten if you find communication doesn't come naturally to your team. The most important thing to remember once again is that process is not the same as outcome. Don't confuse the meetings themselves with the communication that should be happening as part of them. The communication is far and away the most important thing, the meetings are just a way of facilitating it.

Collaboration

Of course, since the way that people communicate isn't the whole story, and neither is the volume of this communication, we must also consider another factor of successful agile implementation, that of collaboration. If I've seen one thing sink agile projects over the years, it's a lack of collaboration. Often this is closely related to a lack of communication, but it is still distinct from it. Communication could theoretically just be a series of people each lecturing each other. It is only in collaboration that the give and take, the debate, the compromise and the mutual understanding emerge. This is why people arguing over agile and scrum so much really annoys me, as an argument may technically be communication, but it very often feels like the exact opposite of collaboration.

There is another watch out to be aware of when it comes to collaboration. If you've built a passionate, excited and communicative scrum team, you still need to make sure that your team are all collaborating in the same direction. As Coram and Boehner note of agile software development scenarios:

"A single strong-willed developer, developers who don't work well together, a customer who doesn't engage with the team, each could destroy the collaborative nature of a group." [59]

This issue often emerges out of the very passions and enthusiasms you've spent time creating within your team. If different members of the team have differing skills and interests in the project, then their enthusiasm could lead them to promote their area of specialism and interest over the areas of others during meetings such as sprint planning, sprint review or just during their day to day work. As Chin states;

"The core team members need to learn to balance their influence on other team members between support of their individual/functional efforts and support of team agility." [60]

A side effect of team members promoting their own areas can eventually be the siloisation of responsibilities, where barriers start to replace boundaries. If someone works on something passionately, it can start to feel like their baby, and so make them resistant to constructive criticism or the involvement of others in their work. Again, practices that are toxic to building an agile culture of team collaboration.

Leadership

---

[59] Coram, M., & Bohner, S. (2005). 'The impact of agile methods on software project management', in *Proceedings of the 12th IEEE International Conference and Workshops on the Engineering of Computer-Based Systems*, pp. 363-370.
[60] Chin, G. (2004). *Agile project management: how to succeed in the face of changing project requirements*, New York: AMACOM. p. 41.

Increasingly then, we're seeing that agile and scrum aren't just things that come about as if by magic, born out of the infallible goodness of people's hearts. In order to stay on track, it all needs some form of guidance, so it is worth considering the role of leadership as a factor in the implementation of agility. But before we do, we must first consider the difference between leadership and its close but different counterpart, the phenomenon of management.

I suspect many don't tend to think too closely about the difference between leadership and management. Managers lead organisations, and leaders manage great projects don't they? Well, possibly at a semantic level, but in reality there is a big difference between management and leadership. As celebrated change management author John Kotter suggests[61], management is concerned with planning, budgeting and organising, whilst leadership is more about vision, alignment and inspiration. If this is true, then looking back at our comparison of agile with the big idea, it appears clear that a move to an agile approach will require management to take a back seat, and true leadership to come to the fore. This may be more difficult than might be expected, for as Kotter states,

"*Success creates some degree of market dominance, which in turn produces much growth. After a while, keeping the ever-larger organisation under control becomes the primary challenge. So attention turns inward, and managerial competencies are nurtured. With a strong emphasis on management but not leadership, bureaucracy and an inward focus take over. But with continued success, the result mostly of market dominance, the problem often goes unaddressed and an unhealthy arrogance begins to evolve. All of these characteristics then make any transformation effort much more difficult.*" [62]

---

[61] Kotter, J.P. (2012). *Leading Change*. Boston: Harvard Business Review Press
[62] Kotter, J.P. (2012). *Leading Change*. Boston: Harvard Business Review Press

Does any of that sound familiar given what we've been discussing in this book so far? The big idea is the victim of its own success, given the degree to which it became able to dominate a stable and predictable environment. The big organisations it has created, from big advertising agencies to big advertisers, have in their turn sought to control their growing numbers of employees and projects, and thus focused inward on planning, budgeting and bureaucracy. In turn, this problem has been allowed to persist due to it still fitting the stable external environment, meaning an arrogance has arisen, one that causes big idea marketers to declare their campaigns a success when the campaign launches, not when its results come in. After all, if you're focused on planning, budgeting and organising, and you succeed at all three to deliver exactly what you specified at the time you said you would for the cost you predicted, then you've succeeded right?

However, as digital and the Internet are drastically changing the external environment, an agile approach is required in response. As covered above though, this approach would require managers to throw away all the practices they know and believe in so firmly; their love of planning, of budgeting, the comfort of predictable, unchanging bureaucracy. It seems clear then that an organisation will not be made more agile through more management, or indeed through those with a managerial mindset. Not only can management not easily bring about change, it has little motivation to do so. Instead, an agile approach requires leadership.

Now, of course there are many different definitions of what it means to be a leader, and many different styles of leadership that can be used. If you only consider leaders to be single great figures, striding out in front whilst controlling everything behind them, then you're really missing a trick, especially when it comes to agile.

---

p30.

As I say, there are numerous definitions of leadership and interpretations of leadership styles, enough to fill up books of their own. For the purposes of simplicity, we need only for now consider the ideas of authors like Cavaleri and Obloj [63], who see leadership as a continuum, with an autocratic work-oriented approach at one end and a democratic people-oriented approach at the other end. When you take this view, it is easy to see that leaders working in agile environments need to be at the democratic, people-oriented end of the continuum in order to be effective. As Bonner observes;

"Because of agile's focus on people and collaboration, combined with the need to embrace change, leadership requirements are vastly different than those using traditional process oriented approaches...a leader's personality profile and way of interacting with others is at least as important as their intellectual ability and 'hard' project management skills." [64]

This comes back again to the point we looked at above, where the personality and inter-personal outlook of the members of the agile team is just as important as the processes and tools they use. Highsmith even goes so far as to argue that as a result, successful agile leadership cannot be taught, and may be an innate quality some people possess and others do not [65].

I would not go this far, for as with all absolute statements of fact, with an agile mindset you can only know they are true once you try them and find out for yourself. However, it is worth bearing these ideas in mind as you explore how leadership works in your

---

[63] Cavaleri, S., & Obloj, K. (1993). *Management systems: A global perspective*. Wadsworth.
[64] Bonner, N. A. (2010). 'Predicting leadership success in agile environments: An inquiring systems approach', *Academy of Information and Management Sciences Journal*, Vol. 13, No. 2, p. 83.
[65] Highsmith, (2004). referenced in Bonner, N. A. (2010). 'Predicting leadership success in agile environments: An inquiring systems approach', *Academy of Information and Management Sciences Journal*, Vol. 13, No. 2, pp. 83-101.

organisation's implementation of agile and scrum. At the most simple level, there is obviously some degree of knowledge that agile leaders can learn. For example, them being confident about the different parts of the scrum process and why they are important is one significant learning. Without it, a non-collaborative team, or a team without an agile mindset, can quickly start to unpick the process and revert back to their respective 'big idea' comfort zones.

Equally, it might be important for leaders in agile marketing to reflect on their leadership style more consciously than leaders in other areas. Again, this is a generalisation in need of further research, but I would argue that marketers are typically confident, outgoing people, often blind to their personal biases and convinced of their own talents, firm in arguing for the solutions they believe to be correct. After all, as we have seen, the 'big idea' approach to marketing has instilled the need for this belief into them over many decades now.

If agile instead requires marketers to develop a servant leadership style, one that is more collaborative and based on coaching rather than instructing others, it may require existing leaders to modify their behaviour significantly. Equally, it may need them to move away from 'big ideas' in leadership itself, a world where their personal brand matters as much as the brand they're working on. Instead, they ought to forget about the big accomplishments for which they can publicly claim credit, and focus instead on guiding from the edges, making a thousand individually imperceptible changes, testing them, seeing which work better than others, and stop looking for the one big change that will make everything alright. As Lao-Tzu said;

"A leader is best when people barely know he exists. When his work is done, his aim fulfilled, they will say: we did it ourselves".

As with many of the factors that influence the success or failure of introducing an agile mindset or scrum process, there are sadly no hard and fast rules around agile leadership, just different aspects for you to think about. However, you may find this list collated by Bonner from reviewing the agile literature a helpful starting point for your exploration, and if you're interested in exploring leadership within agile further, you could do worse than read Bonner's entire article [66].

Agile leaders...

...believe in and trust people to do a good job
...motivate team members to work outside the norm
...provide continual guidance (incremental vs. up front)
...promote connections between people and teams
...influence and inspire rather than coerce
...facilitate group decisions
...cause things to be done (behind the scenes) rather than using authoritarian control
...only intervene when necessary

Honesty and trust

Honesty and trust are two more of those tricky interpersonal agile issues from which people tend to shy away. They're sometimes difficult to discuss openly, but I believe avoiding such discussion can be hugely dangerous, especially in the field of agile marketing and communications.

As Seth Godin memorably said in the title of one of his best sellers, 'All Marketers Are Liars' [67]. His point was that it doesn't matter if

[66] Adapted from Bonner, N. A. (2010). 'Predicting leadership success in agile environments: An inquiring systems approach', *Academy of Information and Management Sciences Journal*, Vol. 13, No. 2, p. 85.
[67] Godin, S. (2005). *All marketers are liars: The power of telling authentic stories in a low-trust world*. London: Penguin.

the things being sold are actually better, faster or more efficient, as long as the end consumer believes the story being told. Now he means this in the sense of marketers talking to customers, but there is a risk that marketers employing this approach when talking to customers will start to employ it when talking to people inside the business too. So regardless of whether the project to implement an agile mindset or the scrum process did or not deliver any concrete improvements and benefits, the project will be declared a success and rewards and promotions will naturally follow. In a situation where everyone is playing this game, you even get the multiplying factor that no-one wants to call anyone else out on their positive spin, in case they too get called out in return.

Needless to say, this is a huge risk to agile. The whole point of working in this way is to have no sacred cows, to promote continual learning and improvement, to fail often, fail fast and achieve ever greater results. If an agile team starts to game the story it's telling to itself or to those around it, a mindset soon sets in that this is acceptable behaviour, and the behaviour spreads into the work of the project itself. Not only do lies contaminate the project, they also erode one of the principles of the agile manifesto, that projects are built around motivated individuals, who are to be trusted. If a culture of lies, spin and half-truths start to creep in, it is impossible to build trust within the team, and the rest of the process starts to fall apart too.

As I say, I suspect honesty and trust are two areas where those wishing to introduce agile into the world of marketing will need to take special care. Not to say all marketers are inherently liars, far from it, but in an industry that spends its days putting that final layer of gloss and shine on so many different products and services, the risk of honesty and trust being corroded is especially great.

Environment

The environment has a huge impact on the successful implementation of agile and scrum. If you start to dig into the literature around agile, time and again the warning emerges that if certain environmental conditions aren't present, your implementation process and subsequent usage of agile will be more difficult, if not impossible. This for me is a big watch out, as whilst we have already looked at many things which can kill off an agile approach, few can do so as permanently as the issue of the environment. After all, you could run the scrum process perfectly, sticking absolutely to the letter of its recommendations, but if the environment in which scrum is operating won't allow it to succeed, then the conclusion tends to be that scrum in and of itself 'just doesn't work'. In fact, the truth is that it only doesn't work because you've kept it in an environment in which it will most likely die. Regardless, it is easier to blame and dismiss scrum and agile than it is to consider what in your environment may actually be killing your attempts to be agile.

However, what do we mean by the word environment in this context? For me, it breaks into three distinct areas: the physical environment (sometimes called the socio-material environment), the organisational-cultural environment, and the wider external marketplace. Let us consider each of these areas in turn. They're not as complex as they sound, I promise.

First, the physical environment is obviously important to agile. We've already looked in depth at the idea of collocation of agile teams, locating each team member in the same physical environment. In addition to this, there are a number of other physical environment considerations that emerge when you start seeing how agile happens in your particular organisation. For example, if agility is all about promoting conversations and collaboration, you need to provide somewhere for these activities to take place. Agile organisations tend not to have meeting rooms people book, they have meeting rooms people just use. Sometimes spaces get used for multiple small meetings, with additional communication and collaboration happening because people are unwittingly having related meetings next to one another. As part of these meetings, people may want to start writing or drawing out ideas for each other during the discussions, and it is noticeable how many teams operating in agile paint one of their walls with chalkboard or whiteboard paint so they can spontaneously draw and write all over them, then wipe them clean and start again.

Equally, if the agile team is encouraged to self-organise and be responsible for how it does its work, why should it not be responsible for structuring its own physical environment too? There has been some interesting research done around how much more creative teams are when they control the environment in which they do their work [68], and it can be no coincidence that some of the most creative and agile startup companies set themselves up in cheap derelict spaces where landlord 'fair wear and tear' provisions are likely to be less stringent, and facilities management departments non-existent. This last point may be a big issue for large marketing organisations wanting to implement an agile approach whilst keeping the office looking 'smart'.

Related to the physical environment is the organisational environment in which an agile mindset is being embedded or a scrum process created. In many senses, this equates to the existing organisational culture and processes into which the new approaches are being introduced. It goes without saying that this organisational environment can have huge impacts on agile and scrum, not least because agile and scrum can have equally large impacts upon existing culture and processes in return. Where the existing environment differs from agile and scrum, there is inevitably a risk of the two clashing. Sadly, in such situations, the existing culture or

[68] See https://hbr.org/2014/01/employees-perform-better-when-they-can-control-their-space/

process invariably wins against the as yet unproven new upstart. We shall return to the problems of organisational change in more detail later, but for now, just be aware that wherever changes to culture and process are proposed, there will be supporters of the status quo who will be actively or passively opposed to them.

This is not to say agile and scrum have to change the organisational culture overnight. For its early phases, agile might be able to sit in relative isolation from the normal way of things, especially if it is being sponsored by someone senior in the organisation. However, invariably some of the differences between the new and the old ways will eventually need to be resolved to mutual satisfaction. Some of the first issues that need dealing with may well be around managing the people who were previously used to having their feedback acted upon, or who were used to being able to alter arbitrarily the prioritisation of the work being done. Reconfiguring project budgets and allocations of staff time might also be necessary quite early on, given the way agile changes the way you think about time and cost. If you find these issues in your workplace, my advice would be to pick the battles that are worth winning, and don't sweat the small stuff. As we saw above, agile leadership is about collaboration and lots of tiny readjustments, so it would be both counter-intuitive and counter-productive for the agile practitioner to demand whole-scale changes to the entire organisation right from the start.

In considering how an agile culture will integrate with an existing organisational culture, it is also worth considering whether the scale of the challenge is just too large for a successful integration to be possible. For example, if you only ever deliver the sort of marketing that has a detailed plan and timeline of future campaigns and assets, each with fixed launch dates, then trying to work with agile might possibly be more trouble than it's worth. This is not to say it wouldn't be hugely beneficial, as in today's turbulent digital marketing environment it can only be of benefit. But it would require the organisation to rethink fundamentally the way it goes about its marketing before it tries to implement agile. Similarly, if every marketing decision has to be agreed by a wide range of senior people, then implementing agile may require them to reconsider entirely the role they play in the campaign process, devolving more decision making down to the frontline where the tests are run and the data is collected.

As mentioned above, you may also have to consider that you may not be trying to implement agile just in your organisation. You may in reality be trying to introduce it across multiple organisations, once you start to include external marketing or PR agencies and contractors in your marketing campaign delivery. This is not impossible, but it is certainly challenging, and may be a decision you wish to weigh up against its timescale. As Chin states:

"Since projects are, by definition, of finite duration, it often doesn't make sense to try to create an agile...environment across multiple corporate cultures. The time and effort required to create the agile culture may not have time to pay off, depending on the length of the project." [69]

The decision as to whether agile is feasibly a fit with your existing organisational culture and processes is one only you can take. However, it is one you have to consider carefully before taking, and tread carefully if you do decide to go ahead. Agile is a fashionable term in marketing right now, but sometimes its most vocal proponents are those who least understand its implications. Do try not to be amongst their number.

Finally, we should remember the environment of the external marketplace in which agile will be used. We have considered this

---

[69] Chin, G. (2004). *Agile project management: how to succeed in the face of changing project requirements*. New York: AMACOM. p. 18.

factor a good deal already in this book, especially in chapter two, where we saw that agile is a great response to complex, fast-paced and uncertain environments, but that it might not be as useful where marketing environments are relatively stable and well understood. Equally you should consider the types of marketing or communications material you're trying to deliver. We shall return to this in chapter nine, but for now, consider how much more iterative, test-driven and data-driven you can be with a digital display banner in comparison with a multi-million pound TV advertising campaign. Ultimately, if you feel that your marketing and PR campaigns are still performing as predictably and as well as ever, then there may be no need to consider moving to an agile approach at all. However, if you're encountering new channels that you're not sure about, and are beginning to get the suspicion that they're channels in which your competitors are stealing a march on you, it may be time to start considering agile.

Chapter 7 - The Problems Of Organisational Change

We've looked then at agile, scrum and 'Big Idea' marketing, and hopefully you're already thinking about how your organisation could change from one to the other. However, we often just think about organisational change as a movement from one state of being to another, a simple phrase for work that can be neatly scoped, planned, implemented and monitored like any other project your organisation may run. In short, the risk is that we start looking for someone who will say:

"Do these things, and you will become an agile organisation"

Now this is a hugely tempting phrase, but in reality it is just a sticking plaster for a vast universe of different factors that may make change chaotic, unknowable, short-term and unpredictable. As much as me giving you a simple 10 step plan to follow in order to guarantee success may shift more copies of this book, to give you one would be a nonsense, and would be against the entire spirit of the agile philosophy this book aims to promote.

Change, if you think about it, covers a ridiculously wide range of topics. For if anything is capable of being changed, then change is capable of being anything. It always surprises me when I hear people referring to an organisational change project, without much reference to what exactly it is that is being changed. Is it the people who work there, making the current ones redundant and bringing in people with the new skills needed? Or are you making no redundancies and instead looking to retrain your current employees? Maybe this isn't about skills at all, and you primarily want to change the organisational culture and mindset. What about the use of power and who gets to exercise it in the organisation? Are you planning on changing that? What about the physical environment too? Where people sit, the quality of their surroundings, the technology they use? Regardless of what is being changed, do you know why things are being changed in the first place? Are you looking to increase employee satisfaction, increase the organisation's profits, win industry awards, or something else altogether? When is this change going to happen? How long will it take?

Change then is a vast topic, and as a result, it is one you should never underestimate. Even if it is apocryphal that 70% of all change initiatives fail, it is still little wonder some do fail, as very often they are run by people with little experience or training in running change, little understanding of the numerous questions we've already identified, and little motivation to change in the first place. After all, if a change project is run by senior people in the organisation who have got where they are thanks to the current status quo, how much change can you realistically expect to occur?

There is also the big factor of time. Think back to the last time you went on an away day, attended a training event or went to a conference that left you feeling inspired and re-energised.

"*From now on*", you vowed, "*I'm going to do things differently*".

That feeling may have lasted a day, it may have lasted a week, but how many of those feelings you've experienced can you truthfully say you still hold today with the same intensity? The problem with change is that it is often harder to keep up the longer it takes. Organisations, cultures and mindsets are all quite elastic things, you can bend them into a different shape for a while, but unless you take real effort to keep them in the new shape, they can soon spring back into the old one.

Sometimes, successful change takes a few attempts before it sticks. Prochaska et al suggest that people going through change programs go through four stages; pre-contemplation, contemplation, action, and maintenance [70]. In doing so, they very often get to the action stage then change back to what they were originally doing, and they may do this three or four times before the change becomes the accepted new way of doing things. Perhaps for this reason, John Kotter suggests that real change can take five to ten years before it becomes an accepted part of the organisational culture [71]. Until the change has become deeply embedded, it is still subject to failure. However, this implies that you know how you will be able to tell that change has become successfully embedded. This may sound like a meaningless truism, but I think it's worth stating that you can only know when your change has been achieved if you know what change you're aiming for. Very often, change projects have lots of noble ambition but very little clear purpose. Gaining 'speed to market' and 'being more responsive' are noble goals, but how do you know when you've achieved them? One option would be to get down to the minutiae of change, set some benchmarks and decree that change will only be considered to have been achieved when '27.9% of marketing campaigns are delivered in three weeks or fewer'. But if you do this, you risk not noticing unexpected but beneficial change that may occur as an unforeseen consequence of the intended change. You also risk preventing the change from changing itself as the environment changes around it. What if halfway through your change project 27.9% of campaigns being delivered within three weeks turns out to be far too slow still, or becomes irrelevant due to a technological change?

All of this, the unknowability of change, the uncertainty of whether it will work, the fact it may not have a definite completion date, the risk of changes in the external environment, they all make change sound like a situation ripe for an agile mindset. One that can adapt to change, explore new environments with low risk and shift direction as new information emerges. For me, this is where it gets

[70] Cited in Weick, K. E., & Quinn, R. E. (1999). 'Organizational change and development', *Annual Review of Psychology*, Vol. 50, No. 1., pp. 361-386.
[71] Kotter, J. P. (1995). Leading change: Why transformation efforts fail. *Harvard Business Review*, Vol. 73, No. 2, p. 66.

interesting, as there is an academic school of thought in the field of organisational change that admits these facts without ever mentioning agile.

The school's main thought runs along these lines. There are fundamentally two types of organisational change that can take place, Type E and Type O. Type E is based on a desire to generate as much shareholder value, basically as much money, from the company as possible. Type O is based on a desire to invest in and increase the organisation's capabilities. Type E is usually a short-term piece of work involving redundancies, restructuring and cost-saving. Type O is usually longer term and involves:

> *"changing, obtaining feedback, reflecting, and making further changes."* [72]

Being long term, Type O change can start to be a continuous process that evolves over time, and as such, you could call it emergent change [73].

Do you notice something there? This whole planned / emergent debate is the same one we've considered before in this book, in the discussion of strategy we had in chapter two. Not only this, but we concluded that agile is the best response to the uncertain nature of today's marketing environment; an emergent approach that best fits uncertain times. However, most important of all, Type O change sounds exactly like it's using the agile mindset, with its lack of emphasis on planning, the way it promotes observation and reflection, and the way it is itself open to change and emergence. In contrast, it is hard to see how Type E change could be used to implement agile. How can you promote a culture of 'collaboration

---

[72] Beer, M., & Nohira, N. (2000). 'Cracking the code of change', Harvard Business Review, Vol. 78, No. 3, p. 134.
[73] Weick, K. E., & Quinn, R. E. (1999). 'Organizational change and development', *Annual Review of Psychology*, Vol. 50, No. 1., p. 375.

over contract negotiation' when budgets are being slashed and people made redundant? 'Responding to change over following a plan' sounds like a particularly cruel way to run an employee redundancy program that may take many months to conclude, and one that will only promote an individualistic rather than collaborative culture.

I would suggest that this fact has quite profound implications for deciding when a change to an agile organisational culture, mindset and methodology is most appropriate. In short, it seems unlikely that it could be run in organisations that have realisation of shareholder value as their single and only goal. In many ways, I think this is ironic, as agile organisations often deliver much greater shareholder value over time, but the realities of the marketplace are as they are. For an organisation to embrace agile, it has to have employee trust, job safety and personal development at the heart of its approach. It must be an organisation that is willing to take the short term hit a change program may cause, in order to realise significant long-term benefits.

So then, perhaps if we want to become an agile organisation, we should treat our organisational change project as an agile project in and of its own right, perhaps even going so far as to run it using scrum methodology. It's an interesting idea, let's explore it in the context of the agile manifesto.

First, John Kotter suggests that change works best when it is emergent in an organisation, perhaps starting with just one or two people, but quickly gathering and involving many motivated individuals to take part [74]. This ties in wonderfully with point one of the manifesto, 'Individuals and interactions over processes and tools'. If your agile change project can quickly bring in many

---

[74] Kotter, J. P. (1995). Leading change: Why transformation efforts fail. *Harvard Business Review*, Vol. 73, No. 2, p. 60.

people to take part in and champion it, the increased likelihood of its success seems a no brainer. As an agile response to this, change becomes all about bringing people together, getting them to communicate as often as possible, ideally face to face, and have them bring in other people to collaborate on the work. Indeed, I suspect this is one of the places where change projects that are centrally led fall down, as whilst the leaders have a clear vision, they are loathe to let anyone else collaborate on this vision and possibly lead it in new directions as the new learnings and knowledge emerge.

For me, this brings us back to the issue we considered earlier, the interesting tension between leadership and management in an agile change process. Weick and Quinn note Kotter in asking:

> *"Is change something one manages or something one leads? To manage change is to tell people what to do (a logic of replacement), but to lead change is to show people how to be (a logic of attraction)."* [75]

Kotter himself adds that:

> *"Management's mandate is to minimize risk and to keep the current system operating. Change, by definition, requires creating a new system, which in turn always demands leadership."* [76]

Clearly then, an organisational change to an agile mindset needs to be done in an attractive way by leaders, rather than a planned way by managers. If change is achieved by showing people how to be rather than telling them what to do, then it sounds very much like the coaching approach that should be taken by a scrum master. As

---

[75] Weick, K. E., & Quinn, R. E. (1999). 'Organizational change and development', *Annual Review of Psychology*, Vol. 50, No. 1., p. 380.

[76] Kotter, J. P. (1995). Leading change: Why transformation efforts fail. *Harvard Business Review*, Vol. 73, No. 2, p. 60.

per agile manifesto principle five, the change leaders should embody motivation, motivating individuals to join the change program and work on it enthusiastically. They also have to have trust in those working on the program with them. If they don't trust the motivated individuals who join the project, then they'll not be embodying the agile change that is being worked towards, and so will reduce their motivation. Worse, the individuals may end up realising that the leaders already believe they know the right answer, and start second-guessing them in their decision making. In this instance, the leaders are making it clear that they don't trust those working with them, and unwittingly lead these people to make far less responsive and feedback informed decisions in the process. As we have seen above, there is once again a clear difference between paying lip service to agile and living its values day to day.

Leaders of agile change, and those motivated individuals who join them, also need to hold true to the mindset of welcoming change over following a plan when it comes to the change process itself. Very often, and with the best of intentions, organisational change programmes set out clear binary differences to illustrate their point. Option A is where we are today. Do nothing and we will stay there. Option B is where we want to get to. Given change is a complex and uncertain environment, just like the digital environment we looked at earlier, people feel tempted to respond to this complexity with simple, knowable binary visions like these. However, to do so is fundamentally non-agile. As Weick and Quinn note;

> *"Replacement of one program with another seldom works. The problem with such a logic is that it restricts change to either-or thinking... (it) precludes the possible diagnosis that both A and not-A may be the problem."* [77]

[77] Cited in Weick, K. E., & Quinn, R. E. (1999). 'Organizational change and development', *Annual Review of Psychology*, Vol. 50, No. 1., pp. 361-386.

There is an important lesson in this. A change program that wants to move from its current state to an agile approach may, in the process of responding to change over following a plan, arrive at the conclusion that agile is not the best approach to use. This, to my mind, is great. If an organisation is not at all willing to make the changes required to implement an agile mindset, or fundamentally does not need to in order to respond to its external environment, then it is probably best not embarking on the agile change program at all.

This is especially true if what Abrahamson says is correct, when he floats the idea of 'repetitive change syndrome'. This has three main symptoms: initiative overload, change related chaos, and employee burnout [78]. We've already considered how chaos can arise in both agile and 'big idea' approaches to marketing, but initiative overload and employee burnout are also two factors very likely to kill agility. After all, as we have seen, agile can potentially lead to increased speed of delivery, but it is more focused on leveling the workload and preventing employee burnout. An agile implementation program that burned employees out in the process would be entirely contradictory. Likewise, initiative overload is opposed to agile, given principle 10 of the agile manifesto, which states:

"*Simplicity - the art of maximizing the amount of work not done - is essential*".

Through this chapter so far, there has been one important thread developing. Agile is a significant organisational change. Done right, it changes the culture, the mindset, the processes and the power relationships within an organisation. As a result, agile is

[78] Abrahamson, E. (2004). 'Avoiding repetitive change syndrome', *MIT Sloane Management Review*, Vol. 45, No. 2, pp. 93-95.

often received with extreme hostility by those it affects. I like to call this ‘prefect syndrome’, as I first encountered it at my old school. In the sixth form, certain pupils were made prefects, and given certain powers over the pupils in the lower years. As a somewhat individual and free thinking person, even at a young age, I often used to find prefects would use their powers on me to get me to conform to the way they thought things ought to be; to conform to the cultural norms. I used to object to this often pointless and arbitrary usage of powers, but whenever I complained, I was told to put up with the injustices and inconsistencies in the current system. As I was told that in a few years I would be a prefect in the sixth form myself, and so be similarly free to use my powers as arbitrarily as I wished.

This seemed wrong then, it still seems wrong now, but it is instructive as to how power relationships emerge in organisations. If those at the top have had to get there through accepting and living with injustices on their way to the top, they are perhaps less likely to be in favour of rewriting the system to become more open, less planned, more trusting and more collaborative. They’ve fought hard to get where they’ve got to, and put up with a lot of pain along the way, so changing the system behind them makes all of that heartache seem less worthwhile. As if it somehow invalidates the things they had come to believe in, invalidates the suffering they put up with, and implies that they had been doing things wrong all these years. Indeed, not only does change feel uncomfortable for people involved in it at senior levels, any change at any level can increase feelings of uncertainty, inadequacy and a desire to stick with what is known than leap into the unknown.

From all of this, we can see that an organisational change to an agile philosophy, or even just a process change to a coherent scrum methodology, is likely to run into many different issues, all of which threaten to delay it, derail it or redefine it completely. However, it looks as though successful change is an incremental process, one that must be explored, reviewed and adapted as new information emerges. It is a process that requires people to collaborate, and to focus on setting and achieving outcomes that add value to the organisation. In short, it sounds like a process ripe for being managed using an agile approach. Now I haven't seen much research into using agile in the field of change management, and to veer off into this field away from using agile in marketing and communications would be an unnecessary distraction for this book. It's an idea worth bearing in mind though, and one I may come back to later.

Chapter 8 - Data

For all we still don't know about how marketing works in the era of the Internet, there's one thing we do know. Regardless of how much we know, we know that more than ever before, the knowledge is there to be found. As touched on in chapter two, one of the key differentiators of marketing in a digital age compared with marketing previously is the issue of data. Thanks to the Internet, marketers now have access to far more data than they ever did, in far more fine grained detail than they used to, and they can access it far more quickly. Whilst a traditional marketer may find this brave new word of data overwhelming and confusing, to an agile marketer, it is nothing but exciting. Not that the agile marketer will necessarily understand what the data means and how to use it any better than the traditional marketer. However, instead of letting the data overwhelm them, they embrace the uncertainty it creates and use agile both to explore it and to understand it better. Let us look in more detail at the issues raised by the increased size, detail and speed of data marketers now have available to them.

First, the increased volume of data is something worthy of a book in and of itself. As with it comes a whole host of different issues. If you're suddenly collecting far more data than ever before, then where do you store it? More to the point, how do you store it securely, given the reputational risk a breach of your customer data may cause? Even if you can store it correctly, how do you store it in a unified manner? It's one thing to have lots of data around how your customers and prospects use the different marketing channels, but how do you tie together the data from those different channels in order to create a single, unified view of their behaviours? This may initially seem like overkill, but one of the holy grails of digital marketing at the moment, one that few have truly cracked, is attribution modeling. If customers are seeing lots of different marketing assets on their path to purchase, and you can tell what these assets were, how do you join up the data to understand the path they took through the different assets? More important, how do you understand which assets performed the best in actually causing the customer to make the purchase[79]? This is where data starts to turn marketers into sales people. Previously, marketers could track things like brand consideration and brand recall through consumer research, but lacked most of the detail on which assets led to which purchases. Now, data such as this is fully available, so does the scale of data fundamentally alter the data we as marketers should care about? Does the line between marketing and sales start to blur even further?

This leads us onto the detail to be found within data in the digital age. Not only are we able to access a lot more data than previously, we are able to access it to a much finer level of detail. Previously, you may have known that a TV ad was likely seen by around X million people. Put the same ad on a digital TV platform that only allows registered and logged in user to watch the programs, and you could in theory know exactly which people saw the TV ad and when they saw it. The level of detail on marketing data has gone from the macro to the super-micro. In one sense this is useful, especially if you can then track the other behaviours of those people, even up until your point of sale. However, if the data gets too micro, then how could you meaningfully make use of it? There are obvious economies of scale in producing marketing assets for larger segments of people rather than producing truly bespoke assets for each person. Equally, there are similar economies from analysing data at a more macro than a micro level. For me, the excitement in this increased volume of data is not in looking at each micro segment of data, the behaviour of each and every individual customers, but how this data can be aggregated together

[79] If you're new to attribution modeling, here's a helpful starter guide from The Drum - http://www.thedrum.com/opinion/2014/09/24/beginners-guide-attribution-modelling

to build a much richer picture of types of customer. Essentially finding the sweet spot between data volume, detail and usability.

This fact becomes especially true once we introduce the third issue, that of speed. No longer do marketers have to wait days or weeks for the research on their marketing activities to come back to them. Now, they can start to see meaningful data within seconds of an asset going live. This is hugely exciting, and allows a much faster and more iterative approach to be taken, continually refining and optimising assets as the data comes in in real time, rather than waiting a long time for the research to be concluded. However, this speed too presents its own challenges. If you're an organisation set up to take the long view on data, how do you refactor the multiple organisation resources and processes set up to handle this reality? How too do you keep sight of the bigger picture when constantly bombarded with huge amounts of fine grained data? It's hard to appreciate the beauty of the sand sculpture when a strong wind is constantly blowing its thousands of grains of sand into your face. If we're not careful, this explosion of data risks paralysing marketers into inaction. It is thus up to the agile marketer to discover how best to make use of this changed new data landscape.

Now of course the interesting thing about data in the context of agile is that the agile Manifesto doesn't explicitly mention it. I'm not certain why this is, but I suspect the answer is twofold. First, in the world of software development, data is so prevalent and commonly used that there perhaps appeared to be no need to mention it explicitly, just as there was no need to remind developers to breathe. For example, if you're coding software, you will very likely write unit tests at the same time as the code; tests which confirm that each element of the code is performing correctly. The results of these tests are obviously binary. The code either passes or fails. The unit test makes no judgment as to how beautiful the code is, or whether the font the code is written in is on brand, or whether the code is the best code the coder has ever written. All of those are human judgments, based on opinion rather than data, not judgments computers would produce. At least, not currently.

Second, and this is where it gets more interesting, is the omission of any specific mention of data in the agile manifesto due to the risks that data can bring with it? Data is a neutral thing, not good, not bad, not interesting, not uninteresting. It just is what it is. It only becomes, good, bad, interesting or anything else as a result of what humans choose to do with it. Surely it is far more important to focus on things like delivering frequent outputs, satisfying customers and maximising the amount of work not done than it is to specify that data must be used, and indeed how it must be used?

You see, for all data is theoretically neutral, it has become a heavily loaded thing over time. Data is what people use to plan, to control, to run through established processes, to performance manage and to fill up numerous documents. Equally, if data is all about interpretation, then marketers emerging blinking from the era of the big idea risk instinctively overlaying their personal opinions and biases on the data that digital creates. Confirmation bias is a huge topic, but it's worth doing some more reading into if you want to spend some time thinking about all the ways great data could be rendered useless by someone who's spent a lifetime holding true to their opinions. All of these things risk being the enemy of agility, so if we are to use data, then we must surely use it carefully, in case we end up slipping back into the world of plan driven big ideas.

Perhaps more so in agile marketing than in agile software development, there is also a moral question here too. If the data marketers are using gives a hugely detailed insight into each consumer's life, how comfortable are consumers likely to be with that? Whilst there have been some great examples of using personal data to deliver personalised customer experiences by some major brands so far, I am sure it is only a matter of time before a more concerted backlash starts to emerge against this. We have yet, as a society, to agree a collective definition of how much we're happy for brands to use our data, and at what point a line of unacceptability would be crossed. One thing is certain though, the reputational damage to a brand caught at the wrong end of such a backlash could very well be significant.

That said, this is not an appeal not to use data, and I believe any agenda for agile marketing needs to have the requirement for prioritising data over opinion clearly articulated within it. Indeed, we should remember that the agile marketing manifesto we looked at earlier has 'Validated learning over opinions and conventions' as its very first point [80]. For me, and I suspect for the authors of that manifesto, this is necessary due to the cultural importance of opinion found within traditional 'big idea' marketing. If we're moving away from the big idea, then we explicitly need to move away from the practice that underpins and causes it, the love of and belief in the personal opinions of marketers. Agile software development doesn't have this cultural history to the same degree, so likely does not have to make the use of data as explicit a requirement as does marketing.

How then do we use this data? After all, all we've looked at so far in this chapter are questions and problems, not solutions for what to do. Let us delay no longer, and move on to some practical considerations of how to use data in the context of agile marketing.

The first point to note is that data is not the same as insight. A friend of mine sums this up wonderfully with the expression:

"Ooh look, this six is a six!"

---

[80] See http://agilemarketingmanifesto.org/

His point is that in and of itself, data is just numbers. Numbers that can exist on their own, or be turned into patterns and pictures, but either of these are still just pretty meaningless numbers unless you add a layer of comprehension and understanding over the top of them. A practice commonly called insight. Now insight seems like a simple enough word, but I believe it is a word we would do well to understand better if we want to be great agile marketers and communicators. For me, insight has three core components.

First, insight is understanding. It is all very well to see patterns in data, but unless you understand what those patterns mean on a human level, how they come about, how they change in response to other patterns, then they're just interesting patterns. Second, insight is believing. We can observe patterns, we can even understand what they might mean, but unless we truly believe what the insight is telling us, then again the insight is meaningless. I suspect this is a common problem for marketers moving to an agile approach. It is simple to pay lip service to data and insight, but often if it conflicts with the deeply held personal opinion you're used to telling everyone about, then you are likely to ignore it in practice. Finally, following on from this, insight has to be actionable. After all, you can know what the data means, understand the customer behaviours and beliefs it is revealing, and believe that it overrides your personal opinions, but all of this is pointless unless you're actually going to do something with the insight itself.

Now, this is easy to say, but potentially harder to do. All of us may want to make the best possible use of data, but fewer of us will know how to do this. Especially if we've been brought up in the old world of big ideas and personal opinions, a world where data was important, but too limited in size, detail and speed to be the number one concern. So how do you make use of data in agile marketing? Overall, this boils down to three main considerations; team size, team culture and team skills.

First then, team size. This one is perhaps the most obvious of the three, as it relates closely to the fact that digital marketing has massively increased the size and detail of the data that is available. At a simplistic level, it seems to stand to reason that the more data you have, the more people you will need to be able to make sense and use of it. Equally, if your data is coming in more quickly, you will need more people in order to be able to make sense of it and use it before the next pattern of data emerges. When data was small, high-level and slow to arrive, making sense of it could be left to a few individuals. Nowadays, data is now at a scale, complexity and speed where maximum value can no longer be gained from it by only a small number of designated marketing planners or data analysts.

To give an analogy, if you think of the amount of data marketers used to be able to access as being the size of a small Welsh hill, then it makes sense that you only used to need a few people to mine it and extract the gold. If your data's now grown to the size of a mountain, if not a whole range of Welsh mountains like Snowdonia, you need as many people as possible to make the most of your gold rush before your competitors mine it out first.

This is especially true if we think back to the definition of insight we just looked at too. If insight is about understanding and actioning the patterns in data, then it is no longer a passive practice done by one group of people and passed across to others. It is an active practice that everyone must get involved in. The increase in the numbers of people needing to make use of data in an agile approach is not then just due to the increased amount of data, but also the need for this data to make it down to the people at the frontline delivering the marketing. Similarly, it must also make it back from the people at the front line to other parts of the business too.

There is also something immensely liberating in this new reality. Involving more people in using your organisation's data means not just that you have more capacity to handle more data more quickly, but that different people will interpret and use data in different ways depending on their immediate requirements. If you've got more data and more detail, then it is very likely that more and more of your internal teams will be able to start gaining value from it. In an ideal world, this proliferation of data shouldn't just require more people to get involved in handling it, it should actively encourage more people to do so, as it enables more of your teams to start to start to gain value from it for their own work. Overall, the old artificial divides that sometimes exist between marketers, PR people, product designers, company accountants and all sorts of other parts of an organisation seem increasingly bizarre in this new data rich digital world.

This brings us on to the next adjustment we'll have to make in this new data rich world. Previously, when understanding data was one team's job, be they brand strategists or media planners, there was no need for anyone else to be able to access the data. Indeed, teams like that often got nervous about letting others get too close to the data at all. After all, they weren't trained in using it like the strategists or planners were, and were surely likely to leap to all sorts of dangerous conclusions if left to interpret the data themselves.

Besides, data is knowledge, and knowledge is power, so culturally why would those in control of it want to relinquish their control and let anyone work with the data in any way they wished? As a result, in the traditional, big idea world of marketing, data often becomes controlled by gatekeepers, people to whom requests have to be made to get hold of data, which then have to be processed and responded to in due course. Now, of course, this sort of behaviour is fundamentally un-agile. It's a process over an interaction, a documentation rather than an output, often even a contract negotiation over collaboration, and it's hardly maximising the amount of work not done either.

As a result, for me, the concept of open data is fundamental to agile marketing. Now, my view of this is coloured by my background in working with the UK's central government as it impressively transitioned to a modern, digital organisation. Back before its digital transformation, data was very clearly a thing the government owned, and to some degree guarded jealously. I remember one time in 2001 phoning Bristol City Council in the UK to ask for a copy of its annual budget, given it didn't yet publish its budget online. The person on the other end of the phone was immediately defensive, asking who I was, who I worked for and why I wanted a copy of it, but eventually they agreed to hand me a single printed copy in a plain brown envelope if I personally came to the Council House to collect it. A few years later, when I started working with local councils and national government departments across the UK, you still occasionally ran into the same attitude. For example I once product owned the development of an online consultation management system that automatically released its data via an RSS feed, so others could build on and make use of the data. When one local authority security audited the system before purchase, they flagged this functionality as a serious security concern. Passing publicly funded and publicly available council data automatically into any system that wanted to help share it more widely? What a risk!

Thankfully, over time, views like these started to look more and more absurd, thanks largely to a controversial piece of legislation, the UK Freedom of Information Act. With this act in place, the numbers of requests for government and local authority information being made grew steadily year on year [81]. Those in

---

81 https://www.gov.uk/government/uploads/system/uploads/attachment_data/file/217

authority began to realise they could either attempt to withhold data, only to look stupid in the press when forced to release it by the terms of the act, or they could just publish everything up front and gain big wins from looking open, accountable and collaborative [82].

Now, this is not to say the picture is entirely rosy. Those working in digital in the UK government are still typically more open and collaborative than those working in others parts of the government, but still, there has been a marked and noticeable culture change around data happen in that sector in a relatively short space of time. The reason for disappearing off onto the slight tangent, is that I believe the field of marketing is going to have to undergo the same sort of cultural change around data that the UK government has had to over the last decade. The change may not be a big in scale or significant in accomplishment, but I am sure it has to take place.

Just as in government, the field of marketing is going to have to tear down the barriers that exist between people and data, whether this is something as simple as giving more people logins to data accounts, or more problematic such as removing gatekeepers from guarding the data as something only they are allowed to work with. Whatever it takes, people right across the organisation must be given direct access to as much data as possible.

Notice I say they must be given access, rather than saying that they must start to make use of data. If you take an agile approach, then you trust your team to do the best job they can. As a result, you shouldn't need to force data down their metaphorical throats. Not only will this put them off using it, it is also more likely to make

---

833/foi-stats-bulletin-q4-2011.pdf

[82] A big credit for this has to go to the too often unsung hero of the modern Internet, Tom Steinberg, and in this case his website https://www.whatdotheyknow.com. Likewise the late Chris Lightfoot, one of the people to whom this book is dedicated.

them pay lip service to it or not fully believe what they are seeing. Data is sometimes uncomfortable for marketers brought up on opinions and big ideas, so if we want and need them to make more use of it, we must use the carrot far more than the stick.

For me, data is exciting. It genuinely transforms the knowledge and insight organisations can bring to their marketing activities, and it is a primary component of any move towards agility too. Far better to excite and interest people into using it, than to sack the gatekeepers by force then order everyone to pick up the gatekeepers' work on top of their existing day jobs. Indeed, I don't for a minute think you should sack your gatekeepers at all, but instead you should persuade them to become facilitators of data, collaborating to help people access it as simply as possible, and facilitating them to make the best use of it.

If you want an analogy, think of what a librarian does. A library would be a much poorer place without a librarian, but librarians don't tell visitors which books they are and are not allowed to read. Neither do they tell visitors which books they absolutely must read. Instead, they proactively help visitors find the books they're most interested in, make sure the books are looked after and are regularly available for other people, even provide visitors good facilities to do reading in too. In a new agile world, your former data gatekeepers need to become data librarians, looking after the data, making sure it is kept in the best state possible, and proactively helping people get hold of the parts of it they need. Their role as a data gatekeeper may be redundant, but their role as a data librarian has never been more vital to their wider organisation.

One final point I'd like to make on this issue is inspired by a quote from Steve Jobs, which reads:

"*Creativity is just connecting things. When you ask creative people how they did something, they feel a little guilty because they didn't really do it. They just saw something. It seemed obvious to them after a while; that's because they were able to connect experiences they've had and synthesize new things. And the reason they were able to do that was that they've had more experiences or they have thought more about their experiences than other people. Unfortunately, that's too rare a commodity. A lot of people in our industry haven't had very diverse experiences.*"

Now here he's likely talking about experiences such as foreign travel, or working in different industries, or studying different academic subjects. However, I believe the same principle holds true of data too. The more data people get to experience and think about, the more creative they are likely to be with it. More research is needed in this area, but I do wonder how much our common perception that data is the opposite of creativity is actually very wide of the mark indeed.

However, as with agile, I suspect there is often an interesting cultural change that happens when you take the approach of opening up your data. The more you open data up, the more you make it interesting to people. If you only ever circulate data in the same formats, then you not only massively reduce the interest people have in it, but also the creative things they can do with it when they're exploring something they're interested in.

Through all of this however, there remains one thing we have not considered. You've opened up your data and got more people excited about making use of it, even turned your gatekeepers into librarians, but what if your people don't know how to make use of data at all? This is a factor I believe to be much more common in the world of agile marketing and communications than it is in the world of agile software development. At the risk of straying into generalisations, software developers are generally logical, mathematical people. They write code that either works or doesn't work, computers that are entirely predictable and free from emotion, and often have a mathematical approach to solving problems. Marketers on the other hand couldn't be more different, steeped in a world of creativity, beauty, personal opinion and the million shades of grey that come with influencing human beings into emotional responses. So making sure that your marketers are equipped to handle the data requirements of an agile marketing environment is of critical importance, far more so than in agile software development.

This is potentially a huge topic, but for now, it boils down into three core requirements. First, marketers have to learn to manipulate and analyse data quickly and simply. This approach comes of course from the agile principle of maximising the amount of work not done. Why bother to teach your marketers advanced statistical modeling with software like SPSS if all they ever really need to do is keep an eye on the total number of engagements on a Facebook post? I've been analysing and reporting on datasets in various different capacities for most of my career, and to be honest, I've never needed much more than a copy of Microsoft Excel and half a dozen different formulas to get all of my data analysis done to a standard I can make use of. This is one of those areas where access to Google combined with regular practice can sort this issue out for you entirely, although some initial coaching is also likely to be useful too.

The second requirement is to keep things simple, and keep most of your data usage closely related to your user stories. Data can tell you all sorts of things, but if you're taking an agile approach, then you're only really interested in the things it can tell you that generate value for your business. The best way to do this initially is to use data to feed directly into your user story approach. This can either be by regularly turning the data into new user stories, comparing new data against existing user stories to see if they're still valid or worth working on, or using data to see if the asset you produced delivered against a user story you have already delivered.

Over time, as your teams grow more confident with using data, their usage of it will likely expand, but providing user stories as a focus for the use of data at early stages can give useful focus and direction to people's data related efforts.

The third requirement is related to simplicity, and is around the area of scope. Traditional big idea marketers instinctively like to think big and strategic, so they will often want to aggregate data together and look for the largest and most visible patterns within it. They will then try to answer these patterns with one single big idea. The trick to avoid this is to keep people looking at the data at a much more micro level, at least initially. Not to say that they shouldn't keep one eye on the bigger picture, but they shouldn't get lost in the sorts of huge, in depth and time consuming data analyses that used to inform long term strategic marketing plans. By keeping data usage on a more widespread but more micro scale, if lots of people just do a small amount of data analysis, and do it quite quickly, then cumulatively you start getting lots of value from your data in double quick time.

However, there is a risk with this last approach, and it lies in the area of simplicity. It's all well and good to keep their usage of data quick and simple, but this should not mean that they only ever make use of the simple data. I believe this happens an awful lot in practice, especially in social media. There's so much data available, and it's flying at you so fast, that you respond by just looking at the data that's quick and simple to analyse. As a result, you get people celebrating how many likes their Facebook post got, or that a topic that they introduced trended on Twitter. These feel like wins, and they're simple to analyse and report on, but do they really meet the agile requirement for the work to deliver real business value? If you trended but no-one spotted that it was your brand behind it, or if you didn't sell one single extra widget as a result, then this great data might be pointless, even misleadingly reassuring. Instead, far more insight and value might come from analysing the comments people posted on Twitter that caused your campaign to trend. Qualitative analysis of free text can take longer to run, and certainly requires more effort than just counting up the likes on a post, but the business value derived from it for a marketer can often be vastly higher. In short, keep your data analysis quick and simple, but always balance this with the business value the analysis actually generates.

So we've looked at the concept of data in the context of digital marketing, the Internet and agile culture change, but we still need to look in more detail at how you use data within the scrum methodology when it is applied to the world of marketing. First up is insight. If insight drawn from data is the cornerstone of an agile or scrum marketing approach, then we should expect to see it feature within the day to day work of a scrum team. Happily, if you remember back to chapter five, you'll have spotted that it already does. To save you referring back to it, I've repeated below the diagram of the agile marketing sprint cycle I propose using.

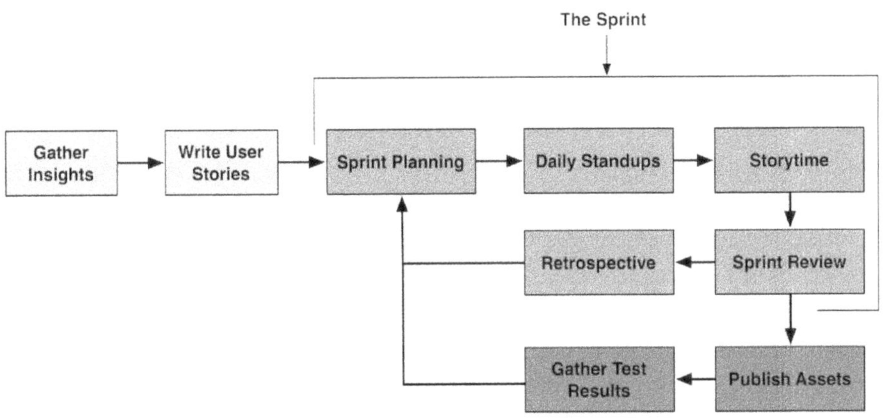

As you can see, my proposed approach to the marketing sprint cycle has two sections outside of the sprint itself. The first is the activity you do in order to write some epic user stories before you get into the first sprint and start producing outputs. I've called it 'Gather Insights', which is a disarmingly small phrase for what can be an alarmingly large process. With the proliferation of data and the speed in which it can change, careless scrum processes can, if they're not careful, initially spend months in a never ending data exploration loop, failing to get started and actually produce outputs. Of course, the better you understand your insights, the better the initial user stories will be, but you should always balance this idea with the fact that many of your most valuable data and insights won't arrive until your sprints start putting marketing assets out there for your consumers to interact with.

This leads us on to the other part of the diagram above that is also outside the sprint cycle, publishing assets and gathering test results. For me, this is the most exciting data and insight that emerges from using agile to deliver marketing. It's one thing to create generalised models of your customers and how they interact with marketing in their day to day lives, but it's much more interesting to see exactly how they interact with and consume the marketing you're producing. Because agile is now letting you produce small amounts of assets regularly, you can start testing ideas over time, seeing how people react, and constantly keep improving performance against your business objectives.

There is though one big elephant in the room when it comes to the issue of testing in the field of agile marketing. Many agile methodologies of course set great store by testing. In the software context however, as we have seen already, testing means something quite unique. As you write code for software, you can also write unit tests for it, automated processes that check that the code is operating as it should. Individually, these tests are reassuring, but collectively, they can save huge amounts of time when building on the software further or fixing bugs in it. As a result of the high esteem in which testing within software is held, it is a substantial part of many agile methodologies, if not the philosophy itself. Indeed, in a software environment, the QA stage of the scrum board shown in Chapter five often has a very different meaning. In software, a card may be in QA whilst the automated tests of that feature are evaluated, and then automatically moved into done once the tests are all passing.

However, in marketing, we have no such testing. How do you write an automated unit test for the content of a video on Youtube? You can't, as computers can't yet understand beauty, personal opinion or brand guidelines. The only testing that can be done before a marketing asset is set live is to let others evaluate it and comment on it. This is fine to a degree, but, as we've looked at already, it runs the strong risk of killing your agile project and mutating it back into big idea marketing with its personal opinions. To avoid this, agile marketing has to have a very different emphasis than agile software development when it comes to testing.

For agile marketing, a huge part of the emphasis on testing should be on testing the outputs with their intended target audiences. In essence, setting them live and seeing what happens. This is not to say software developers don't do something similar, and aren't equally as interested to see how end users use the software they build. However, for them, testing is often an automated process in which end user reaction is a secondary source of data. For agile marketers, little to no automated testing exists, so the emphasis has to be on end user reaction.

The thing is though, where do you start incorporating this test data into the scrum process? In software development, it would sit in the day to day work of the sprint, and perhaps be reviewed in the sprint review meeting, checking the tests pass before agreeing that an item on a card is done. In agile marketing, I believe this approach should be different, with test data being fed instead into the sprint planning meeting. There are two reasons for this. First, the test data on the outputs of the sprint is fundamentally not available by the time of that sprint's sprint review meeting. It will only become available once the assets have been put live amongst consumers. You could of course include the data on the assets from the previous sprint in your sprint review, but what would be the point of that? Why waste time looking at data from a completely different sprint to the one you are reviewing?

Instead, I believe test data in agile marketing should be fed back into sprint planning meetings. If you incorporate data into your sprint planning, you get a number of benefits. First, the team as a collective can understand more clearly why the product owner is prioritising the stories in the way they are, and understand that over time, this prioritisation is more and more likely to be following the successes they are creating. Second, the team can understand the stories and the tasks that may flow from them more clearly. If testing has shown that one approach is an absolute banker when it comes to a type of marketing asset, then they can identify it as a strong one to test and improve even further. Finally, through the mere fact of making test data a part of the sprint planning meeting, you're keeping your data driven approach at the forefront of people's minds, and so part of their daily habits. For example, if people are disagreeing about a route to take in sprint planning, get them to work collaboratively on testing each approach to see who is right.

Of course, to say data in agile marketing goes into the sprint planning meeting does not mean it should not be used at other stages of the sprint cycle too. Storytime sessions can be hugely enhanced by comparing the stories in the product backlog against the latest test data you are getting back. Similarly, the product owner may want to review test data when they're prioritising the stories in the product backlog, which they are free to do at any time. Even team members may look at, interpret and use test data in their day to day work of delivering the items on the cards on the Kanban board. As we looked at above, if agile requires open data, then we cannot specify that it will only go into certain meetings or stages of the scrum process. It can go wherever it likes, there are just some meetings, like sprint planning, where it definitely shouldn't be absent.

Finally then, let us look at the lowest level of the usage of data, the day to day work of running and reporting on tests. As with other sections of this book, there are many blogs, articles and books out there that will help you with this, but for now, let's just stick with a top level overview. For if it excites you, you can go out and Google it. If it doesn't, at least I'll have helped you find that out. That said though, to my mind a marketer would have to have a cold, cold heart and an entirely uninquisitive brain not to get at least a bit excited by testing marketing assets. For the more testing you can do, the more you can speak from a position of authority. Whilst others around you are thinking that something might perhaps happen, the more you actually test that thing and learn from it over and over again, the more you can speak with increasing certainty. After all, as mentioned above, data is knowledge, and knowledge is power.

How then, in simple terms, does testing work in agile and scrum based marketing? Well, the approach I usually take is all about what's called A / B testing. In essence, putting out two different versions of a marketing asset and seeing which one of them performs the best according to the data. You then take down the one that performs less well, and leaving the winner live for either the rest of the campaign, or until it gets beaten further down the line by a new, better performing asset. Whilst this approach is a micro level one, it is also important to keep an eye on the macro level too. Constantly reviewing the results of all of the individual A / B tests being run, using them to shape the future development of your work, aggregating them into meaningful insight that might, just might, one day become a big idea or proven best practice [83].

How then do you run an A / B test? Typically such tests follow these 7 stages.

1. Have question
2. Do research
3. Write hypothesis
4. Design test
5. Launch test
6. Track and monitor results
7. Do analysis and write up results

Let's look at each of these stages in turn.

---

83 I still think best practice is largely a meaningless term in the complex, uncertain and ever changing digital marketing environment, but I do believe there is a chance that we may, one day, finally settle upon some.

1. Have question

All good tests start with a question you want to answer. For me, this is about both parts of that statement. Good tests start with a question, and that question should be one you or your team actually wants to answer. Questions for tests can come from all sorts of places, but if the people running the test aren't especially interested in the answer, they're much less likely to do a good job of it, making the test deliver less value than you hoped it would. Indeed, a test run incorrectly could produce misleading data that takes you off down a dark alley, wasting time on doing the wrong thing. Alternatively, you could run a test perfectly, but if you've no interest in the answer, then you won't actually learn anything from it. Often it's better not to run a test at all and save the money than to run it badly and waste even more money as a consequence.

2. Do research

Once you've thought of a question you're interested in, do some research into it. Just as the scrum meetings provoke much more communication amongst the team, your testing process can provoke much more learning. Sometimes, research helps you or the team refine the question even further, including elements that hadn't been considered. Sometimes the research answers the question completely, removing the need to run the test at all, which is an even more efficient win than running the test itself. However, there is a slight risk in this approach, given that whilst the research you do may answer your question, the information used for the research may have become out of date over time. Never be afraid to run a test again if you suspect you may get a different result to the one the research may suggest.

3. Write hypothesis

This is the part of testing people very often miss out, but to my mind, they really shouldn't. A hypothesis is what narrows your question down into something you can actually test, and it takes the form of a statement which is either true of false. For example, 'a marketing message promoting the product's quality will have a higher click through rate than one promoting its price' or 'a direct mail letter containing one phone number will generate more phone calls than a letter containing three'. There is no limit to the number of hypotheses you can create, and they give you a simple, core focus to the tests you then design.

4. Design test

Once you've turned your question into a hypothesis, you need to design your test. Now, there is a huge number of ways you could design the test, and a huge number of factors you may need to consider, but the most important thing to watch out for is making it a true A / B test. Unless you're a statistical whizz at doing multi-variate testing, then essentially you should only change one thing in the test. So for example, if you're testing messaging, then change only the message on the marketing assets, but keep the design, the colour scheme, the size, the placement, even the time the two assets will be live all the same. Minor variation of factors other than the one being tested are sometimes not the end of the world, but as soon as you start changing more than one factor, you're quickly moving into dodgy ground. Stick with one change, keep things simple, and keep the tests and the learnings moving at a rapid and responsive rate.

5. Launch experiment

Once your test is designed, get it live as quickly as possible. Create the assets, set them live, keep moving, keep learning. Big idea marketers may want to step in and refine the assets based on their personal opinion. After all, having personal opinions about things and making last minute changes is what they've been brought up to believe senior marketing positions are all about. Unless they have a screamingly good reason to do so, don't let them. If needs be, classify them as a blocker and call in your scrum master to get them out of your way.

6. Track and monitor results

Once the test is live, start looking at the results it is generating. Whilst you don't want to call the results of the test concluded until you're confident they've become stable through gaining a large enough sample size, looking at the data early and often has a number of advantages. First, it gets you excited. This may just be me, but personally I can't wait to start looking at the data when the test goes live. This is one of the reasons that choosing questions you and / or your team are genuinely interested in is so important. The sooner you start looking at the data, the sooner you can start thinking about what it might be showing you, and start to see if the patterns you're noticing carry on or disappear over time. If a pattern is consistent right from the start of the test to the end, I'm usually pretty confident it's giving me a firm answer. However, and this is another reason to start looking at the data sooner rather than later, it may be that the data is looking way off what you expected, or isn't even being recorded in the way you expected. This can happen, and could signal that the test has either been designed or delivered incorrectly. If this does turn out to be the case, it's better to stop the test early, adjust it and run it again than let it run its course and end up with unusable or incorrect data.

7. Do analysis and write up results

This part of the testing process can be huge, deep and involved, or quick, informal and punchy, or somewhere in between. Personally, I prefer the quick and punchy approach. If the test, and the optimisations it brings about, are ultimately meant to be delivering value to the business, then the less time between the end of the test and the roll out of the optimisations, the better. This is not to say you would not at some point look at the test results in more detail, but it is better to do this periodically, and often by aggregating the results of a number of tests together to see if any larger patterns are occurring. Run, analyse and learn from each test quickly, but occasionally take some time out to run a deeper analysis that generates multiple learnings.

As we can see, taking this approach to testing essentially involves rapid incremental exploration, each time generating new knowledge and continuous improvement, just the sort of thing agile marketing should be all about. Through regular testing and course adjustment, you could find over time that all of your small pieces of work aggregate up into a big idea. One with all of the benefits a big idea can bring, but one built on proven data, constantly optimised and delivering value to the organisation. Pretty sweet huh?

Chapter 9 - How Far Could Agile Spread In Marketing?

So then, we're nearly at the end of our journey through the world of agile marketing and communications. It's only a first visit to this world, because this book itself is being written in an iterative and agile way, with hopefully a number of future versions to come. It seems fitting then to round our journey off with a discussion of some new territories we may want to explore; some areas for further research. If enough people are interested, I'll see if I can upgrade this section in future releases. If not, it will grow more slowly, or even be cut out all together.

What I want to do though, is offer a brief exploration of how agile might apply to different areas within marketing. I am aware that the book thus far has looked at agile marketing from lots of different angles, but has by and large avoided looking at whether some channels in and of themselves allow marketers to be more agile than other channels do. For example, whilst you could clearly write some Facebook copy using scrum, could you really produce an agile TV ad in the same way?

As we've considered throughout this book, agile is still hugely new to the world of marketing. As a result, not enough useful case studies have yet risen to the surface to help us map out the likely limits of its applicability. Indeed, if you think about it, how many are likely to surface anyway? Agile promotes working software over comprehensive documentation, so how many truly successful teams are going to spend lots of time writing about their work [84]?

However, this book has set out lots of different elements of agile marketing that are in need of further research. One hugely important area for further research in agile marketing is the

---

[84] I am aware of the irony inherent within the author of a book on agile writing this statement...

environment in which agile and scrum are being implemented. Fundamentally, different types of marketing activity create very different environments around them. So let us now look at each marketing channel and consider how agile and scrum may or may not work in trying to make use of it.

Television advertising

TV adverts, the holy grail of big budget, big idea marketing, giving those frustrated feature film makers who have ended up at advertising agencies the chance to create their own beautiful, emotionally charged mini epics that win them awards, and occasionally also sell a few products or services at the same time.

I joke slightly, but there is this slightly monolithic quality to TV advertising. It's expensive, and can undeniably have vast reach and result in huge impact. It's the thing everyone gets to see, and is generally the cornerstone of any very large marketing campaign. Running TV ads is thus largely the preserve of the 'big boys' in any given industry, although this is not to say there is not huge variation in cost and scale even within this sector. A Superbowl half-time TV ad or UK Christmas ad for a high street retailer may be a seven figure budget talk of the town, but smaller companies can get access to TV advertising on smaller channels at less watched times of the day too. Still, even the companies doing this still tend to be the bigger players in their particular field. To look at it another way, TV advertising is unlikely to be the first marketing essential sought out by a bootstrapping start-up company using a Lean Startup approach. As such, TV feels inherently un-agile. It costs a lot, is often based around a big creative idea, takes a long time to produce, and you don't get the scale, detail or speed of data that you can get in more digital channels.

So, could you ever use agile or scrum for delivering a TV ad? Certainly there are a number of things that probably could make the transition across. For example, on the face of it, working more collaboratively is likely to be a benefit for any type of marketing activity you may wish to look at. However, we must remember that whilst agile is about valuing certain types of activity and behaviour more, it is also about valuing other types less. Perhaps due to its scale, perhaps just due to its origins and longevity, TV advertising is a practice that still places value on the right hand side items in the agile manifesto, the things agile values less. Whilst any TV advertiser may say they are keen to do left hand side activities such as focusing on outputs, responding to change and building collaboration, are they really willing to devalue their existing processes, tools, documentation, contract negotiation and following of a plan with that much money and reputation at stake?

Besides, how iterative can you really be with TV anyway? As we have considered at various points in this book, the point of running a process like scrum is to start delivering value quickly, and keep on delivering it steadily, regularly taking a read of the data that becomes available and adjusting future phases of the work accordingly. TV at the moment feels like a much more Waterfall based media, with large fixed budgets, firm deadlines and necessarily sequential production stages, including script writing, storyboarding, shooting, editing and distributing.

Despite this, there might be some mileage in exploring how you could break the different stages of the delivery process for a TV ad down to work in sprints. For example one sprint spent writing the storyboards, another sprint doing the filming and a final sprint doing editing. However, you would still be lacking customer feedback on how your activity was performing until the TV ad went live, and even then you might not get a meaningful read on the data for a month or two post launch. You're iterating, but you can't shape and adapt the outputs of those iterations based on data. Basically, TV advertising is currently the big idea writ large.

However, I think a more interesting angle to explore here is how an agile approach might turn TV itself on its head. Agile may be a more flexible and responsive approach to the uncertainty of digital channels, but aren't digital channels themselves now changing the nature of TV? At the time of writing, here in the UK the BBC is taking the hugely successful BBC3 off the air and making it a digital only channel, accessible through the Internet. At the same time, 300 hours of video is being uploaded to Youtube every minute[85]. Anecdotal evidence suggests that young people no longer care much about TV schedules, as they expect to be able to watch whatever they want to watch, whenever they want to watch it. If we're talking about TV advertising in a digital age, then we must accept that TV advertising itself is changing; away from the big budget Saturday night primetime slots, and towards catching people's attention on Youtube before they click 'Skip Ad'.

Now, I suspect you could create these types of digital TV advertisements using agile and scrum. You can produce them for less money and effort, you can get them live more quickly, you can get a read on their performance data much earlier, and if they're not working, you can just take them offline again and put something else in their place. As a result, you can run more of them, more often, target them at individual audiences, even do A / B testing on them. This is an area for further research, but my initial feeling is that we should not be discussing how we run traditional TV advertising using agile and scrum, we should be asking how agile and scrum help us understand how the Internet is reshaping traditional TV advertising itself[86].

---

85 http://www.youtube.com/yt/press/en-GB/statistics.html

86 For an interesting example of this, check out http://www.bbc.co.uk/taster. The BBC is testing stories quickly online, and if they don't work then no great loss, if they do work, they'll take them further. A classic agile approach to developing TV content, definitely one to watch.

Print ads

I feel sorry for print advertising, I really do. For years and years, large circulation newspapers and magazines could charge big money for advertising space within their pages, knowing that advertisers had few other options that would give them the reach and resonance newspapers could offer. Then, circulation started falling[87]. Across the world, print newspapers and magazines are being bought and read by fewer and fewer people, with many titles going to the wall as a result. Of course, this has not necessarily meant the death of the newspaper, as many of them have moved online, and after a few false starts, they are now finding ways to monetise their online presences, either by charging small amounts for access to content held behind paywalls, or instead relying on generating traffic to the pages in order to sell impressions and clicks on digital advertisements to advertisers.

For the purposes of this discussion, we shall consider print advertising as separate from digital advertising, even if both are being carried out by the same organisation for functionally similar reasons. Like TV, print advertising has a number of issues with adopting an agile approach, although the likelihood of success does seem greater. In theory, print ads can be produced quite quickly and cheaply. As long as a slot is available, a simple and quick bit of artwork could get knocked together in a morning, filed with the newspaper before the print deadline for the next day, and be sitting on breakfast tables across the country the next morning. Often production costs for print ads are higher than those for digital display ads, but I suspect this is more an artifact of history than a modern necessity[88]. Regardless of the production cost however, the

---

[87] For an interesting analysis of this see http://media-cmi.com/downloads/CMI_Discussion_Paper_Circulation_Trends_102813.pdf

[88] Look at the print advertising of budget airline Ryanair. They made a virtue of producing print ads as cheaply as possible, even getting their staff to take the photos for the adverts using cheap cameras.

distribution cost is likely to be relatively high, with significant wastage from a great many different causes.

However whilst distribution may be relatively expensive, with potentially low production costs, you could likely run A / B testing on print ads, putting out different versions with a unique response mechanism on each version. Typically this would involve putting a different phone number on each variation of the ad, so you could tell which version of the ad any given sales phone enquiry had been caused by, then add the results up to see which ad performed best. Despite this possibility, it is undeniable that in comparison with digital display advertising, the data available through print advertising is pretty Stone Age. With digital display you can tell who looked at your ad, what other ads they had looked at before, how many times they look at your ad, their age category, their gender, their location and many, many other variables. With a print ad, you can know where it was distributed, and find out who gets in touch with you because of it, but other than that, you're pretty much flying blind. So what would be the value of using a scrum approach to develop print ads? With print circulation ever falling, you have to wonder how much longer an agile approach to delivering print advertising could continue to justify the business value it returned for its cost. As with TV, an agile approach to print advertising would question whether print advertising was still worth continuing in its current form.

Radio ads

If TV advertising is big, time intensive, expensive and monolithic, then radio advertising often seems to be anything but, at least to the listener. I admit I'm not old enough to know whether there once were glory days of radio advertising, but despite having listened to or appeared on the radio regularly since 1992, I've never heard any radio advertising that didn't sound slightly cheap and cobbled together. Perhaps it's the lack of non-verbal communication you get with radio compared with TV advertising, or the need for radio ads to fit in in amongst recordings of music rather than TV programs, but radio advertising has never felt quite as monolithic as TV. It is also interesting to note here that there has been a plethora and diversity of radio stations for longer than there have been lots of different TV channels. Perhaps the larger number of stations led to greater ease of access and so more marketers using radio as a channel than TV.

Whatever the reason, whilst radio could be seen as a stable and predictable platform to which a big idea approach may be suited, it has two important qualities that quite possibly mean it could more easily adopt an agile approach than people may at first realise. First, radio is increasingly a digital channel. RAJAR figures in the UK suggest that DAB digital radio usage has risen from around 5% to 25% since 2007, and the usage of the internet, apps and digital TV for listening to radio has also been increasing steadily too[89]. The more radio becomes just content that is distributed through digital channels, the better suited it will be to an agile approach, for all of the reasons explored in this book so far.

I suspect there is also potentially an interesting cultural angle to the radio industry that may inform the adoption of agile and scrum for delivering marketing via radio. Whilst TV has always been a one-directional push based channel, where marketers publish messages for audiences to consume, radio has in fact long been a two way channel, much more akin to social media. As someone who has often presented radio shows, I know that being a radio DJ can be a lonely experience. Talking into a microphone for hours with no-one joining in with your conversation feels unusual. As a result, radio stations have long mastered the art of consumer conversation, getting their content consumers to phone in to the show, whether to

89 Data retrieved from http://en.wikipedia.org/wiki/Digital_radio_in_the_United_Kingdom#/media/File:UK_digital_radio_listening.png on 26/4/2015

win prizes or join in the debate, and increasingly now to text in, email in, tweet in and whatever other channel in too. As a result, I'm not sure the radio industry will find agile quite as alien a concept as the TV industry might. This is not to say the transition will necessarily be any easier, but I do believe the opportunity is more clearly there with radio than with other traditional channels.

Billboard posters

If ever evidence were needed about how much marketing has already changed over the last few decades, billboard posters are a great source for it. I remember back in the 1990's when Wonderbra's 'Hello Boys' billboard campaign buried itself in the national consciousness by basically showing a massive image of a woman in her knickers and bra on roadside billboards across the country. Have we seen anything so impactful done with billboards in the last decade? I very much doubt it. So the first thing to say about the use of agile in delivering billboard marketing is that it might cost more than the value it returns, given billboards in many ways appear to be a dying media anyway.

Not only this, but of all the media out there, billboards seem to rate the lowest in terms of other prerequisites for agility. Being static pieces of information that just sit there 24/7 until they get covered over by another ad, you can't know who saw them, when they saw it, which one they saw, or anything much at all. You could put a different call to action in each one and try to use that to track their performance, but even then, you'd have trouble building them into an accurate attribution model alongside the digital elements of your campaign. So overall, I'd say agile and billboards is not a growth area right now, and neither is it one that is likely to make agile implementation easy, so I'd perhaps suggest leaving it alone.

That said though, the same applies to billboards as it does to other traditional media. It is not just that digital is superseding billboards in importance, it is also that digital is fundamentally changing what billboards are. Increasingly, old static poster based billboard sites are being replaced with large digital screens, and the range of technology you can use in conjunction with them is growing too. For on digital screens, you can set messages live as quickly as you can create them, meaning they can be far more relevant to context, time of day, likely audience and all sorts of other adaptable and testable factors. Technology is also developing that can sense smartphones in the near vicinity, and use the data on them to target individual messages at individual people as they walk past the digital screen or billboard. This technology is likely only to keep advancing steadily over time. So again, a discussion of agile in relation to this channel highlights the degree to which digital is fundamentally transforming what the channel now means and the role that it performs for marketers. As such, it sounds like a very likely candidate for an agile approach indeed.

Email

Following on from this discussion about 'billboards', whatever that term may now mean, we can see a similar pattern happening with email. Email is the product of a channel that has already been through the transformation that billboards are now experiencing. For in the traditional days of marketing, direct mail, physical objects posted to people's homes and places of work, was the one-to-one channel that marketers had to use. As with other traditional media, direct mail like this was to some degree harder to iterate and easier to use with a big idea. However, it did have the advantage over a billboard advertisement, that whilst a billboard is one asset that thousands of people walk past, a direct mail campaign produces thousands of assets, each one individually posted to a specific person. As such, the scale and variability could be there for iterating and running A/ B tests. Although the main barrier to such an approach is the difficulty in gaining performance data back from the end recipients. Similarly, it would of course be far more costly to send 10,000 bespoke letters, each individually tailored to the specific interests and demographics of 10,000 different people, than it would be to write one letter and print it 10,000 times. In direct mail, a big idea might not be absolutely necessary, but it's certainly easier, cheaper and more tempting to do.

Email of course has fundamentally altered this dynamic. Because it's removed any printing costs, and because it's also allowed data to be merged into copy automatically, the cost and complexity of sending 10,000 different messages have now both massively reduced. Similarly, the collection of performance data has massively increased too. I don't know if you're aware of this, but each time you receive an email newsletter, it is very likely that the organisation sending it can track exactly when you open it, how many times you open it, which links you click on within it, who you forward it to and many, many other variables besides. As such, the email marketing industry often feels like one of the most advanced when it comes to practices such as A / B testing, and massively lends itself to an agile marketing approach. Indeed, if you were looking to see whether agile marketing might suit your organisation, you could do worse than running it as a pilot to deliver some email marketing, such is the close fit between email and agile practices.

Digital display

Digital display is an interesting digital marketing channel. On the one hand it's huge, and now responsible for funding and keeping afloat many journalistic endeavours that would otherwise have sunk long ago. On the other hand, it's a digital industry that often feels like it's been captured by the big idea marketers. If you see a digital display ad once, you're likely to see it a dozen times, and the ads are often all about interrupting your online experience and desperately trying to grab a few seconds of your attention. If you're the sort of marketer that's used to TV advertising, then digital display can look suspiciously like TV too if you're not careful.

But could digital display be delivered using agile and scrum? Of course it could. Some of the data you might hope for may not be as prevalent as you might wish. Various stats fly round the web about unlikely sounding things you're more likely to do than actually click on a digital display ad [90], but fundamentally, thanks to tracking cookies, the data you need to iterate and adapt is very much there.

The need for agile might also be much greater in digital display than in other channels too. Increasingly, display ads are being sold programmatically, meaning essentially that the decision about which ad is shown to you is only taken within the few milliseconds of you arriving at that web page. Not only is this decision taken at the last possible moment, a good agile principle, it is also based on a huge range of data the site detects about you and your browsing habits when you first arrive at the page.

As such, the range of assets needed for successful programmatic digital display marketing is potentially huge, as is the range of data you can receive back in return. On top of all this, digital display is still a relatively new and changing marketplace, complex and uncertain, making it ideal for delivering using an agile approach.

PPC

PPC, or Pay-Per-Click advertising, is basically making sure your website appears near the top of Google's search results when people search for words relevant to your business. However, I'm always uncertain whether marketers deep down believe that it is

[90] http://www.thewire.com/business/2011/06/you-are-more-likely-survive-plane-crash-click-banner-ad/39429/

actually a marketing activity. On the one hand it definitely raises awareness of your business, drives traffic to your web pages, and often converts into sales. On the other hand, there's very little creativity within it, the PPC ads themselves being little more than a few short words in a fixed font on a white screen. There is also tons and tons of data that can be gained from PPC, and hundreds of permutations that can be run, each targeting different search terms, meaning that it can often be far better delivered by a talented mathematician than a creative marketer.

Now of course all of this means it is absolutely ripe for adopting an agile delivery approach. The data is near instantaneous, the permutations are multiple and the industry is still relatively new and uncertain. However, the question for me is more whether it should be delivered using a specifically agile marketing approach. For whilst PPC definitely helps marketing campaigns, how much is it really akin to what we commonly understand by the practice of marketing?

Social media

If ever there were a channel that lent itself well to using agile and scrum, it's social media. All the prerequisite factors are there, the data, the potential for customer feedback and collaboration, the speed to market and the creativity too. Whilst I disagree that the 'Oreo's Superbowl Tweet' example everyone currently cites as being 'agile marketing' actually was agile, I don't think it's any great coincidence that it was a phenomenon that took place on Twitter.

Of all the digital channels, social media often feels the most uncertain, the most chaotic, the fastest-paced, the most complex and the most unpredictable. It's the place where millions of people can all talk to each other simultaneously, a phenomenon that has never existed in the entire history of human existence on this planet. On top of this, the relationship between customer value and marketing activity is probably closer in social media than in any other marketing channel. It is hard to argue that a TV ad gives value to its end consumer, beyond maybe some minor and temporary entertainment. What's the 'So that...' part of a user story for a TV ad? Social media content however typically needs to demonstrate real value to its end consumer far more clearly if it is to reap the benefits of the channel such as social sharing, commenting and dialogue. Most great social media content I see has a clear user story shining out of it straight away.

So yes, I'd argue that it is a no brainer for social media marketing to be one of the first places you'd look to implement an agile marketing approach. It also has the benefit of being such a different thing that preconceptions of it have yet become quite as fixed as they have done in other channels. Digital display can be confused with TV advertising, podcasting can be confused with radio advertising, but social media marketing really is like no other channel that has existed previously.

The only caution I'd offer in rushing to use an agile approach for social media marketing is around the issue of customer collaboration. If agile is about collaboration, then this needs to be extended to your customers on social media. Merely iteratively producing content, pushing it at customers and collecting data on their reactions to feed into future sprints is not enough, and is also potentially risky. Social media is inherently a social thing, full of real humans displaying real reactions and emotions [91]. If your customers start to feel like you're iteratively testing marketing assets on them in order to optimise them over time, you will likely lose any authenticity and credibility you had in the channel, and do yourself more harm than if you'd just not adopted an agile approach in the first place. Once again, it is the agile mindset you

[91] For more on this, see www.gezsmith.com/book

hold when running these activities that matters far more than merely following an agile process.

Chapter 10 - Conclusion

As I said in the introduction, this book is not the end of the story for using agile approaches to deliver marketing, PR and communications activity. It is merely the end of the beginning, a first attempt at examining the issues currently surrounding these fields, and how agile may be suited to them. So what have we learned so far?

Well first of all, I think it's pretty clear that the fields of marketing, PR and communications have experienced a huge amount of change over the last 10 to 15 years, thanks to the rise of digital and the Internet. The number of different channels people have to deal with has grown rapidly. The speed with which channels rise and fall has grown ever faster, as has the speed at which content within the channels rises and falls too. On top of all of this, the vastly increased number of human connections and interactions has led to a huge amount of complexity and uncertainty with which communications professionals are at times finding hard to cope. Digital and the Internet are changing previously linear relationships between communicators, media suppliers and consumers into multiple different two-way and interconnected relationships. In short, the environments in which marketing, PR and communications have to be carried out have become much more complex, fast-paced and uncertain.

Agile philosophy and its associated methodologies have, at least in the field of software development, found themselves to be well suited for dealing with this complexity, uncertainty and fast pace. From our discussion and exploration in this book, and through my own first hand experiences, it seems they can indeed be carried across to deliver marketing and communications activity with a great deal of success. However, to say this is early days for the use of agile in these fields is an understatement. There is still so much to try out, so much to learn, so much potentially to adapt and shape in order to transfer a software development methodology into a means of delivering marketing and communications.

Throughout the book, I've been flagging potential areas for further research, so it seems worthwhile to list them all in one place here. Are there any of them in the list below that you'd be interested in knowing more about? Are there any that you already have knowledge of or experience in that you'd like to share? Please do get in touch and let me know if so.

- Why do people in the marketing and communications industries automatically think agile is all about speed? Is it just a simple misconception, or does it point at a greater need for something to provide rapid speed and responsiveness in these fields than in the field of software development? Should the implementation of agile in marketing, PR and communications look to shape itself in such a way that it prioritises speed as well as sustainable pace? Is a sustainable pace more suited and relevant to software development than communications?

- Following on from this, are there situations, cultures and environments into which agile should not be introduced? Not just because it will not be relevant to every situation or environment, but because there may be some situations or environments in which agile adoption is necessarily doomed to fail. I suspect there are not, but there might be some instances where the environment or culture might need to be changed so fundamentally and comprehensively that in effect agile is being introduced into a whole new situation. Is there a way we can start to spot these sorts of situations, for example through using models such as Theory E / O organisational change?

- What about online virality, those memes and messages that get shared far more widely and with much greater impact than their creative or media budgets alone could have delivered? Is it the case that such success generally originate from low budget, ad hoc and fundamentally agile people, collectives and organisations, rather than marketing and PR departments with big teams, big budgets and years of industry experience? If so, what does this tell us about the structures and resources needed for agile marketing?

- Scrum may work as a methodology for implementing agile in the fields of marketing and PR, but what of the other agile methodologies? There are many of them, and to my knowledge, few of them have been tested in marketing and PR. Is there a better agile methodology than scrum for delivering marketing and communications work? Could just some elements of the methodologies be taken and adapted, for example using a pair programming approach for delivering real time social media content during specific events? I've deliberately missed out what are know as acceptance criteria and definitions of done from the scrum and user story elements of this book, as I currently believe that they are just too open for abuse by marketers wedded to hierarchy and big idea approaches. Is this an omission too far? Should they be added back in?

- How do user stories work for delivering different types of marketing and PR activity? Can they be applied beyond content based approaches? Do they work for activity that only holds value for the originating organisation, rather than value for the end consumer, such as a TV advertisement? Is the proposed change from user stories to job stories worth considering in these fields too?

- A slight spin off from the main theme of this book, but how much could agile be used for delivering organisational change programmes in and of themselves, regardless of whether they relate to the marketing department, the PR team, a software development team or any other field? If change is an emergent process, and agile facilitates emergence and discovery, is there a whole field of agile change management out there to explore?

- Is data actually not the enemy of creativity, but instead the facilitator of it? Does adopting an agile approach in marketing and PR mean that those skilled in interpreting and understanding data should move across into more creative fields, and those from creative fields should take evening classes in data analysis and interpretation?

- Agile is sadly often prone to arguments. There are all sorts of reasons for this, many of which are to do with the inherent inability of agile to be tightly defined and specified, being much more a philosophy and a mindset than a strict set of rules. By its very nature, it must evolve and adapt over time and in different environments, so some degree of debate and discussion is inevitable. But to what degree have the vehement and unpleasant agile arguments noted by some authors been caused by the prevalent personality profiles of those naturally drawn to software development? Will agile in marketing, PR and communications contexts more likely avoid the arguments because people in those industries are naturally better communicators?

- If agile is a mindset and a philosophy, how fundamentally and how much will the dominant cultures and the big personalities in the marketing, PR and communications industries need to change in order to adapt? Will advertising and PR agencies stop being named after individual people, and start putting forward a more collective and collaborate face, built on their teams rather than their senior managers?

- How much do awards ceremonies in marketing and PR contribute to inagility in these industries? Should those wishing to adopt agile be boycotting award ceremonies and focussing instead on celebrating strong performance data? Do we need to start celebrating and sharing failure more than success? Would we be happy to share our performance data openly with others in order to enable this?

- Whilst much of its content is as applicable to PR and communications more generally, not just marketing, this book has admittedly looked mostly looked at agile in the context of marketing more specifically. How much do the ideas and lessons within this book apply equally to felds such as PR? Is PR is faster paced anyway, and if so, has it already created or adopted its own versions of agility to use on a day to day basis? If so, it would be fascinating to explore these further.

So then, dear reader, it's over to you. There are lots of questions still to be answered, lots of areas still to explore. I shall continue to do so myself, and develop this book over time. However, developing the ideas within it collaboratively with others would be far better, and we'd all benefit from it. So if you've ideas, knowledge or experience to share, or if there are areas and topics you'd like to see explored in more detail, please do get in touch. It would be lovely to hear from you, just email gez@bunnypicnic.co.uk.

www.ingramcontent.com/pod-product-compliance
Ingram Content Group UK Ltd.
Pitfield, Milton Keynes, MK11 3LW, UK
UKHW020130250726
13967UKWH00002B/572

9 780957 275423